These new critical essays on *Wise Blood*, Flannery O'Connor's explosive first novel, not only question our understanding of the "Southern Gothic," but launch a new inquiry into the nature and history of O'Connor's critical reputation, at a time when the construction of literary history is so conflicted. Perceived as a "classic" American writer despite the double setbacks of being a woman and a twentieth-century author, O'Connor continues to speak with striking clarity and disturbing vision to successive generations. Thus far, however, most critical interpretations of *Wise Blood* have been written in much the same key, focusing on the theological strength of its themes and the major character, Hazel Motes. These essays break the monotony of this critical treatment by holding the novel up to the light of several new and controversial methodologies.

The collection begins with Michael Kreyling's explanation of the nature and history of O'Connor's literary reputation using quotations from her letters, works, and from critical reviews and articles covering the history of her presence in the canon. Four critical essays, alluded to in the general introduction, then take up the novel from four distinct and often controversial points of view. Robert Brinkmeyer, Jr., who has written on O'Connor from a more or less traditional theological view in the past, writes a reevaluative essay from that point of view. Patricia Yaeger writes a feminist/psychoanalytical essay exploring the construction of the narrative voice in *Wise Blood*. James Mellard links O'Connor and Lacan, exploring territory that O'Connor herself found dangerous and irresistible: psychology and psychoanalysis. Lance Bacon, finally, writes one of the most original essays in print, placing O'Connor in the milieu of her times, American popular culture of the 1950s.

NEW ESSAYS ON WISE BLOOD

*   The American Novel   *

GENERAL EDITOR

Emory Elliott, University of California, Riverside

New Essays on Wise Blood

Edited by
Michael Kreyling
Vanderbilt University

CAMBRIDGE
UNIVERSITY PRESS

Published by the Press Syndicate of the University of Cambridge
The Pitt Building, Trumpington Street, Cambridge CB2 1RP
40 West 20th Street, New York, NY 10011-4211, USA
10 Stamford Road, Oakleigh, Melbourne 3166, Australia

First published 1995

Printed in the United States of America

Library of Congress Cataloging-in-Publication Data
New Essays on Wise blood / edited by Michael Kreyling.
p.   cm. – (The American novel)
Includes bibliographical references (p.   ).
ISBN 0-521-44550-7 (hc). – ISBN 0-521-44574-4 (pb)
1. O'Connor, Flannery.   Wise blood.   I. Kreyling, Michael, 1948–
II. Series.
PS3565.C57W536   1995   94–17425
813'.54 – dc20   CIP

A catalog record for this book is available from the British Library.

ISBN 0-521-44550-7 hardback
ISBN 0-521-44574-4 paperback

Contents

v

Contents

5

The Woman without Any Bones: Anti-Angel Aggression in
Wise Blood
PATRICIA SMITH YAEGER
page 91

Series Editor's Preface

In literary criticism the last twenty-five years have been particularly fruitful. Since the rise of the New Criticism in the 1950s, which focused attention of critics and readers upon the text itself – apart from history, biography, and society – there has emerged a wide variety of critical methods which have brought to literary works a rich diversity of perspectives: social, historical, political, psychological, economic, ideological, and philosophical. While attention to the text itself, as taught by the New Critics, remains at the core of contemporary interpretation, the widely shared assumption that works of art generate many different kinds of interpretation has opened up possibilities for new readings and new meanings.

Before this critical revolution, many American novels had come to be taken for granted by earlier generations of readers as having an established set of recognized interpretations. There was a sense among many students that the canon was established and that the larger thematic and interpretive issues had been decided. The task of the new reader was to examine the ways in which elements such as structure, style, and imagery contributed to each novel's acknowledged purpose. But recent criticism has brought these old assumptions into question and has thereby generated a wide variety of original, and often quite surprising, interpretations of the classics, as well as of rediscovered novels such as Kate Chopin's *The Awakening,* which has only recently entered the canon of works that scholars and critics study and that teachers assign their students.

The aim of The American Novel Series is to provide students of American literature and culture with introductory critical guides to American novels now widely read and studied. Each volume is devoted to a single novel and begins with an introduction by the volume editor, a distinguished authority on the text. The introduction presents details of the novel's composition, publication history, and contemporary reception, as well as a survey of the major critical trends and readings from first publication to the present. This overview is followed by four or five original essays, specifically commissioned from senior scholars of established reputation and from outstanding younger critics. Each essay presents a distinct point of view, and together they constitute a forum of interpretative methods and of the best contemporary ideas on each text.

It is our hope that these volumes will convey the vitality of current critical work in American literature, generate new insights and excitement for students of the American novel, and inspire new respect for and new perspectives upon these major literary texts.

Emory Elliott
University of California, Riverside

NEW ESSAYS ON WISE BLOOD

Introduction

MICHAEL KREYLING

ABOUT fifteen years ago, opening his review of *The Habit of Being* (1979 [henceforth *HB*]), a selection of Flannery O'Connor's letters, Robert Towers was startled "to recall that Flannery O'Connor would be only in her mid-fifties if she were alive today" (3). It is only a little less startling today, almost three decades after the writer's death in 1964, to realize that she would be "only" seventy this year, quite young enough to enjoy (if enjoyment is in fact a plausible description for what O'Connor might have felt) the veneration, awe, controversy, and simple hoopla that swirls around her life and work. I think she would have enjoyed it all. She wrote to one of her friends: "I seem to attract the lunatic fringe mainly" (*HB* 82).

You can, for example, buy a coffee mug with a cartoon of O'Connor baked into the glaze. She stares out at you with heavy-lidded seriousness, holding a Christian Bible and backed by the spread tail of a peacock – her trademarks. Text on the mug ticks off the major points of the O'Connor myth. She died young of a particularly sinister disease, systemic lupus erythematosus. She lived most of her thirty-nine years (1925–1964) in Milledgeville, Georgia, with her mother, Regina Cline O'Connor, on a farm called Andalusia. "Her stories [are] violent, bizarre, and teeming with metaphor and symbolism," the mug continues. One of them, unnamed on the mug but well known to her many readers, has to do with "a reluctant atheist who puts his eyes out with lye [sic] and walks around with gravel in his shoes." It's lime Hazel Motes rubs into his eyes – but the myth can tolerate small errors of fact.

It is characteristic of our fin de siècle, this smothering of the real with licensed merchandise "tie-ins." O'Connor was just a few decades early with Haze Motes and *Wise Blood* (1952). If she were alive today, a 40th Anniversary Edition of the novel, complete with a marketing package, might well have brought her wealth she would not have been too old to enjoy. Her mother survives. If Flannery O'Connor had inherited her blood instead of her father's, carrying the susceptibility to lupus. . . .

As a sort of commemoration of the nonevent, this volume of "New Essays" on *Wise Blood* appears. It has been assembled not to reinforce the consensus on O'Connor's literary reputation, but to shake it a little out of complacent habits. In his indispensable essay on the state of O'Connor criticism, Frederick Crews ruefully predicts that in "the current iconoclastic mood of academic trendsetters . . . , O'Connor's stock is due for what Wall Street calls a correction" (146). Crews does not undertake the correction himself, and he assesses those who do (some of the contributors to this volume) with a skeptical eye. But it is my belief that methodological and theoretical experimentation does more good for the life of literary discourse than the repetition of a certain set of formulaic phrases that merely impersonate understanding. Without innovations in reading her work, O'Connor would become so familiar as to disappear, leaving only coffee mugs and a few tired phrases.

But the establishment of this monolithic O'Connor industry is instructive in its own right, and it is useful to read the novel with some sense of the canonical reputation it seems to have launched. In general two causes seem uppermost in the list of reasons. The first is that O'Connor's fiction is so rewardingly teachable. As Crews points out, O'Connor was taught to write fiction in the New Critical tradition, and it is therefore no surprise that the rest of us also taught to read that way should find her fiction so accessible (145). O'Connor herself never made a secret of her methods. She recommended the foundational New Critical textbook, Brooks and Warren's *Understanding Fiction* (1943), as a "book that has been of invaluable help (*HB* 83, 283) whenever she was asked for advice. Moreover, O'Connor sent virtually everything she wrote (including every draft of *Wise Blood*) to Caroline Gordon for editorial approval. Gordon, a novelist herself, was also one of the underacknowledged builders of practical criticism out of the general tenets of New Criticism. The editorial apparatus in *The House of Fiction* (1950), which she co-edited with her husband Allen Tate, is almost all Gordon's work. O'Connor was in thrall to Gordon's counsel, and Gordon undertook, in a few critical comments, to direct critical responses to O'Connor along New Critical (and Christian) lines. The reading, teaching, and learning of O'Connor's fiction is stuck in the New Critical gear, and the essays in this volume aim to wrest our habitual response into unfamiliar rhythms.

The second reason why O'Connor's fiction is interpreted with such solid consensus is that almost no one doubts her own testimony as to its Christian meaning. Crews again puts his finger on the problem. One of the earliest critics to point out and dissent from the stringent religious message in O'Connor's work was the novelist John Hawkes, who suspected in 1962 that O'Connor was rather too enamored of the Devil she professed to warn her readers against. His essay triggered several responses defending the writer (of which more later in this introduction) and, quoting Crews, "The Hawkes–O'Connor debate has not subsided in the quarter-century since O'Connor's death. It is the vortex into which nearly every other question about her work gets inevitably drawn, and there is never a shortage of volunteers to replace the original antagonists" (156).

The result of these serial autos-da-fe is nearly five decades of repetitive affirmations of the theological message believed to inform O'Connor's work, reinforced by the tacit belief that her considerable suffering crowned her word with a special truth status. Interestingly, early reviewers of *Wise Blood,* those who read it as a first novel by a young, unknown woman from Georgia, were quite skeptical of the religious power of its characters and message. As the O'Connor persona gained greater circulation, the prestige of *Wise Blood* has grown until it looms as one of the most significant religious novels in American literary history.

Wise Blood, and all of O'Connor's other work (a surprisingly slight oeuvre for such a reputation: *A Good Man Is Hard to Find* [short stories], 1955; *The Violent Bear It Away* [a novel], 1960; and *Everything That Rises Must Converge* [short stories], 1965) are usually seen as instances of the same metaphysical "vision." As Christian tradition interprets the Bible as expressing one Word in each and all of its many parts, so is O'Connor's fiction given a similar unity, wholeness, and transcendental authority. The essays in the current volume tend to question this process and accretion.

"Fiction doesn't lie, but it can't tell the whole truth"

Flannery O'Connor, through her control of her own image as writer, as Southerner, as Catholic, as woman, and so on, still controls our understanding of her life and that life's connections with the work. She was not unaware of the critics' hunger for biographical detail. In 1956 she wrote to "A," her anonymous correspondent:

> Fiction doesn't lie, but it can't tell the whole truth. What would you make out about me just from reading "Good Country People"? Plenty, but not the whole story. Anyway, you have to look at a novel or a story as a novel or a story; as saying something about life colored by the writer, not about the writer colored by life. (*HB* 158)

Even that conceded "plenty" has been underappreciated by her readers and critics.

Mary Flannery O'Connor was born in Savannah, Georgia, in 1925, the only child of Edward Francis and Regina Cline O'Connor. The writer's father died of lupus in 1938. O'Connor remembered her father's death with a sort of tight-lipped stoicism. To the poet Robert Lowell, she wrote: "My father had it [lupus] some twelve or fifteen years ago but at that time there was nothing for it but the undertaker" (*HB* 57). The family was in Milledgeville, Georgia, at the time, the hometown of her mother's family, where they had moved to take advantage of job opportunities during the Depression. O'Connor completed high school and college in town, showing a talent for drawing cartoons and a penchant for mordant commentary on the social rigors of growing up. She wrote to "A":

> This pride in the tin leg comes from an old scar. I was, in my early days, forced to take dancing to throw me into the company of other children and to make me graceful. Nothing I hated worse than the company of other children and I vowed I'd see them all in

4

hell before I would make the first graceful move. The lessons went on for a number of years but I won. In a certain sense. (*HB* 145–46)

Flannery O'Connor took a Master of Fine Arts in creative writing at the University of Iowa Writers' Workshop. For several months in late 1948 and early 1949, she worked at Yaddo on her novel, *Wise Blood*, which had won the Rinehart-Iowa Fiction Award in 1948. From her letters in these early years of professional writing, it seems that O'Connor was determined to make that life in New York. After Yaddo she lived in New York apartments and in rural Connecticut with Robert and Sally Fitzgerald. After a falling out with Rinehart, which was committed to publish the novel, O'Connor took the manuscript to Harcourt Brace. While awaiting publication, in the winter of 1950–1, she came down with the symptoms later diagnosed as lupus. She returned to Milledgeville and, except for short trips away from home, lived there for the rest of her life.

I am doing fairly well these days, though I am practically bald-headed on top and have a watermelon face. I think that this is going to be permanent. (*HB* 55)

No one denies the significance of systemic lupus erythematosus (SLE) on O'Connor's life and work; few hazard a guess at what the particular pathology of the disease (and the treatment) did to O'Connor's fiction. In most critical statements, we seldom get beyond the obvious: living with a terminal disease made O'Connor more sensitive to the meanings in life. "What you have to measure out," she wrote to Robert Lowell, "you come to observe closer, or so I tell myself" (*HB* 57). One of those meanings must have impressed O'Connor, who was a connoisseur of irony: she had become one of her own grotesques.

When she learned that she had SLE, the most virulent form of a spectrum of lupus conditions, O'Connor must also have learned that she had a 40 percent chance of surviving three years after the diagnosis. She must also have known that she was in for a particularly painful and disfiguring disease. Her first symptoms were the fatigue and arthralgia (aching in the joints) common to SLE. She had also to worry about the characteristic butterfly lesions across the bridge of the nose and cheeks, and additional sores on the arms, back, neck, and other parts exposed to light. Like AIDS, which it resembles in some general ways, SLE makes a public spectacle of its victims, turning the body into a vivid display of illness. The figuring on Parker's back, in the last story O'Connor was to work on before she died, might owe something to the Kaposi sarcoma-like lesions some lupus sufferers have endured.

There was also hair loss (caused by the disease and by some forms of treatment), problems with blood chemistry, kidney problems and the possibility of renal failure (this was to be, in fact, the immediate cause of death in August 1964), and the specter of psychiatric and psychological problems. The treatment — in the first years of O'Connor's life with lupus — could be as bad as the disease itself. The state of the art in the early 1950s called for treatment with ACTH (adrenocorticotrophic hormone, derived from the pituitary glands of pigs). The side effects of ACTH, a steroid, were unwelcome: swelling of the fatty tissues of the body (often in the face); deterioration of bone; loss of muscle tone; tumors (O'Connor went to the "cutting table" just before her death [*HB* 567]); insomnia; fatigue.

At one time or another in her life with lupus, O'Connor suffered all of these pains. While her dosage of ACTH was still being adjusted, O'Connor suffered severe joint pain and muscle loss in her legs. She wrote to "A" about her acquaintance with crutches:

> I am learning to walk on crutches and I feel like a large stiff anthropoid ape who has no cause to be thinking about St. Thomas [Aquinas] or Aristotle. (*HB* 104)

One thinks of the paternal wise blood of which Enoch Emery boasts; it also led him into an apesuit. Six months later, x-rays revealed what appeared to be permanent loss of bone in the hip joint.

> I'm informed that it's crutches for me from now on out. Putting a cap on it [the bone] won't be possible because the bone is diseased. So, so much for that. I will henceforth be a structure with flying buttresses. . . . (*HB* 151; ellipsis in original)

Although there was remission in 1958, after a trip to Lourdes (post hoc, propter hoc O'Connor did not decide), she continued to suffer bone problems: she broke a rib coughing too strenuously (*HB* 306) and two years later, in 1960, the bone deterioration resumed in her jaw.

Like that of many AIDS sufferers, O'Connor's suffering was acute and acutely public; her body wore its disease for all to see. She could hope for no happiness through the body. For many critics within the consensus, to argue that O'Connor's use of the body means the flesh in general, and is part of her religious vision, seems only part of the issue. The new essay here, by Patricia Yaeger, explores the condition of the female adult body as one of the preconditions of meaning in *Wise Blood* – without the religious or metaphorical escape hatch.

Flannery O'Connor died in an Atlanta hospital on August 4, 1964; she was thirty-nine. In the thirty years since her death, her life and work have fueled an industry that rivals that of William Faulkner. When the Library of America published her *Complete Works* (1988), she became the first woman and only the second resident of this century (Faulkner had preceded her) to be so publicly canonized. There are now several dozen booklength studies of her work in print – as yet there is no biography – and several hundred articles. National and international conferences meet to discuss her work. No Southern writer (possibly no other American writer of this century) is the subject of so many masters theses and doctoral dissertations. A first French edition of *La sagesse dans la sang* is quoted at $175. And, of course, there is the collectible merchandise.

If we know so much, why do we need more? Isn't *Wise Blood,* the first of O'Connor's two novels, so well known that a good percentage of literate Americans, reading of the "reluctant atheist" who did penance by filling his shoes with rocks, could accurately identify the protagonist of the novel, Hazel Motes? The problem is precisely that familiarity. There has been so much criticism of O'Connor and of *Wise Blood* in so relatively brief a time (as literary reputations go) that the orthodox line is narrow, deep, and resistant to revision. This volume of four "new essays" exists to open new ways of seeing and understanding the novel, and the critical establishment that guards the meaning. We assume that you have read the novel, so we engage in no plot synopsis.

"My background and my inclinations are both Catholic. . . ."

It is a commonplace of O'Connor criticism, originating almost at the start, that her Catholic faith is central to her meaning, and that if a critic ignores, mistakes, or objects to that faith she or he will arrive at distortion and error. To begin otherwise than with Catholic "vision" is to be, as John Hawkes intimated, of the Devil's party. O'Connor never allowed a grain of doubt on this issue.

Early in 1954, in response to a letter of appreciation for *Wise Blood*, O'Connor wrote:

> My background and my inclinations are both Catholic and I think this is very apparent in the book. Something is usually said about Kafka in connection with *Wise Blood* but I have never succeeded in making my way through *The Castle* or *The Trial* and wouldn't pretend to know anything about Kafka. (*HB* 68)

She knew enough, though, to tease her mother:

> Regina is getting very literary. "Who is this Kafka?" she says. "People ask me." A German Jew, I says, I think. He wrote a book about a man that turns into a roach. "Well, I can't tell people *that*," she says. (*HB* 33)

There was less teasing about Catholicism. There were those who believed, or claimed to, and they could be manhandled. But there was always, beyond and untouched by the world, the truth. O'Connor wrote to "A":

> I think most people come to the Church by means the Church does not allow, else there would be no need their getting to her at all. However, this is true inside as well, as the operation of the Church is entirely set up for the sinner; which creates much misunderstanding among the smug. (*HB* 93)

And:

> But I can never agree with you that the Incarnation, or any truth, has to satisfy emotionally to be right (and I would not agree that for the natural man the Incarnation does not satisfy emotionally). . . . There is a question whether faith can or is supposed to be emotionally satisfying. I must say that the thought of everyone lolling about in an emotionally satisfying faith is repug-

nant to me. I believe that we are ultimately directed Godward but that this journey is often impeded by emotion. . . . To see Christ as God and man is probably no more difficult today than it has always been, even if today there seem to be more reasons to doubt. For you it may be a matter of not being able to accept what you call a suspension of the laws of the flesh and the physical, but for my part I think that when I know what the laws of the flesh and the physical really are, then I will know what God is. We know them as we see them, not as God sees them. For me it is the virgin birth, the Incarnation, the resurrection which are the true laws of the flesh and the physical. Death, decay, destruction are the suspension of these laws. (*HB* 99–100)

This lengthy passage makes clear one important grounding for the religious vision of O'Connor: she preferred to see the empirical world – the world of the flesh, of the body – as a set of symbols for the metaphysical. The "true laws of the flesh and the physical," in her vision, were precisely those that seemed to the unredeemed eye to be wishful and spiritual: virgin birth, Incarnation, resurrection. The "actual" or "everyday" existed: out of it you made art. But it existed as a set of signs only, indicative of a Divine Presence: a Reality over and above reality. O'Connor operated, as many critics maintain, on the anagogical level not the historical.

O'Connor's type of belief was to remain constant throughout her life and her work. Even under the assaults of lupus and the equally devastating treatment, she maintained that the "glorified body" of the resurrection was the real body, not the sorry flesh one carted through history. This view could, to some critics, make O'Connor seem hard or mean, but she herself rested serenely in possession of the truth. She felt no allegiance to the cause of human beings trying to make life better for themselves. In 1959, for example, she wrote to "A" on the subject of the Church's stand against birth control:

The Church's stand on birth control is the most absolutely spiritual of all her stands and with all of us being materialists at heart, there is little wonder that it causes unease. I wish various fathers [i.e., priests] would quit trying to defend it by saying that the world can support 40 billion. I will rejoice in the day when they say: This is right, whether we all rot on top of each other or not, dear children, as we certainly may. Either practice restraint or be prepared for crowding. . . . (*HB* 338; ellipsis in original)

9

Very early on, the critics took up the challenge of O'Connor's stern faith and made it the passageway to *the* understanding of her fiction. Robert Drake, in *Flannery O'Connor: A Critical Essay* (1966), writes that O'Connor has come to call the wicked to repentance, especially "modern intellectuals" who have foresworn Christianity and its traditional values (15). *Wise Blood,* Drake asserts, is just such an emphatic call; if it falls short of perfection, it is only because it is deficient in art: "her shattering perceptions about fallen man have not sufficiently coalesced into a strong thematic design" (18). The spirit, in other words, is willing, but the artistic flesh is weak.

This stubborn tradition of seeing O'Connor's work, especially the first novel, as theologically exceptional – entitled to a truth status over and above that which we accord "mere" literature – has overpowered nearly every other approach. Sister Kathleen Feeley's *Flannery O'Connor: Voice of the Peacock* (1972) links O'Connor's technique and meaning to the narrative traditions of the Christian Bible; the blindness and sight tropes of *Wise Blood* are directly linked, for example, with similar tropes in the New Testament (4). Feeley's reading carries the added authority of Caroline Gordon, who acted as O'Connor's chief literary guru during the latter's life and wrote a foreword to *Voice of the Peacock.* Gordon, addressing the charge that O'Connor used too much violence in her plots and too many freaks in her casts of characters, claims that she did so "because they [the freaks] have been deprived of the blood of Christ" (x). Technique and meaning, profane and sacred, are merged in the criticism of O'Connor.

John R. May's *The Pruning Word: The Parables of Flannery O'Connor* (1976) claims the privilege of the sacred for O'Connor's work – and for those who participate in the criticism of it, as long as they do so with good hearts. O'Connor, May contends, always knew the truth, but critics have had to work by a process of dialectic toward a vital consensus that coincides with the author's vision. The critical process May describes is similar to that by which the Bible is progressively interpreted toward the divine truth. In both cases, O'Connor and the Bible, "validity in interpretation" can be guaranteed because the text under study is divinely inspired:

> The reader has no choice [May states] but to hear the universal language of *homo religiosus* spoken by her contemporary parables, and no valid interpretation of them can avoid at least the literary analogues of their basic religious language − poverty, possibility, and judgment. (xxv)

In the sort of reading represented here by John May, Hazel Motes is the prophet brought low in order that he might make an acknowledgment of his own spiritual indigence, the total inability of human efforts in achieving salvation (129); without Christ he cannot save himself. Nor can we: this is the truth borne by O'Connor's writing.

The habit of reading O'Connor as a chosen religious voice, of course, makes some attempt to include the traditional literary aspects of her work: imagery, symbol and metaphor (even the coffee mug allows that), plot, allusion. Suns become consecrated hosts; blind characters represent (or feign) unredemption; repetitions in patterns of three echo biblical calls to the prophet or Peter's denial of Christ. The mechanics of her writing are many, but they can be reduced to one, and the religious vision runs through it. Perhaps this fervent style of reading O'Connor reaches its apogee in John F. Desmond's *Risen Sons: Flannery O'Connor's Vision of History* (1987). Desmond claims that O'Connor's literary achievement is distinguished by a metaphysics that makes the reader/critic's work sacramental. Here is his premise:

> Moreover, I assume her metaphysics, historical vision, and artistic technique all derive specifically from her belief in Christ's Incarnation and Redemption of human history − a belief which, ideally, made her historical sense and her artistic sense inseparable within the creative act. How this unity can be seen developing and operating in her stories will be the main burden of my study. (3)

Desmond's position is virtually a New Criticism turned sacred; the unity he claims for O'Connor's work ("Flannery O'Connor's fiction is all of a piece. Probably more than any other American writer of her generation, she managed to create a coherent wholeness of vision and form." [12]) springs from a theological source − O'Connor's belief in the Incarnation. If there is a vulnerable text, one like *Wise Blood* for example, in which the desired unity is marred by ambivalence or ambiguity in the referential matrix, then the work is marked down to immaturity (59).

Wise Blood and its author were not always so exalted, or was the religious meaning so triumphant. When the novel was originally published (1952; a tenth anniversary edition with O'Connor's brief prefatory note was issued in 1962 – the latter text is the one we usually read), not everyone was floored. O'Connor was a little-known Southern writer vying for attention with William Faulkner, the recent Nobel laureate; Erskine Caldwell, who had patented freaks from Georgia; and Truman Capote, poster-child for the Southern Gothic. When *Wise Blood* saw the light of day, Daphne du Maurier's *My Cousin Rachel* was number one on the *New York Times* bestseller list; Ralph Ellison's *Invisible Man* was number nine.

Reviews did not seem to promise such eminence for *Wise Blood*. Isaac Rosenfeld, no cordial friend to Southern books (he had confessed in his review of Eudora Welty's novel *Delta Wedding* [1946] that he couldn't finish reading it), seems to have read O'Connor without the scales falling from his eyes. He saw no reason to make a distinction between "religious striving" in the characters and simple "mania." Hazel Motes, far from being a prophet in Rosenfeld's eyes, "is nothing more than the poor, sick, ugly, raving lunatic that he happens to be" (19). O'Connor was unperturbed (*HB* 39). R. W. B. Lewis, in an omnibus review for *Hudson Review,* saved two paragraphs for *Wise Blood* at the end of his piece, suggesting that Kafka not Christ was the influential power behind the novel (145, 150). O'Connor, as we have seen, volleyed the Kafka shot right back. Oliver LaFarge in *Saturday Review* found Hazel "so repulsive that one cannot become interested in him" (22). No one can be right all the time.

Just a few years later the battle for O'Connor's reputation (and for the soul of modern literature) had swung to her partisans. In an issue of *Critique* (1958) devoted to O'Connor's work and that of fellow Catholic J. F. Powers, Caroline Gordon took on the competition one at a time. Capote's "freaks," she argued, were merely items in a "case history," not players in a serious study of literature and religion; Capote lacked "moral judgment." Even Faulkner, the great Oz of modern literature, was no contest. His lack of acquaintance with Christian doctrine, Gordon pointed out, "renders his technique infirm"; she called *A Fable* to the bar (8–9). The persistence of this argument can be seen in the repetition of it in Desmond's *Risen Sons* (20–3) thirty years later.

Those who, as Frederick Crews has observed, wish to take O'Connor without her full complement of theology might be doomed to failure. But that does not stop us from trying. Two recent critical works exemplify the ongoing engagement with O'Connor's theological vision. Marshall Bruce Gentry, in *Flannery O'Connor's Religion of the Grotesque* (1986), takes O'Connor at her word when she claims to write from the standpoint of the Christian orthodoxy (3). But Gentry nevertheless tries to secularize this view by reconciling it with Mikhail Bakhtin's theory of dialogism. He sees this as necessary because the end of the fiction (the truth of the Christian message) seems at odds with some of the means (the grotesques – with whom, Gentry accurately supposes, few of us would eagerly identify). Bakhtin's theory enables Gentry to claim that the grotesques are actually positive inasmuch as individually they outdo the grotesquerie en masse. Taulkinham, for example, capital of the grotesque-as-modern in *Wise Blood,* serves as the negative grotesque against which Hazel works out his salvation by forcing himself (and others) to become aware of his grotesqueness. Mrs. Flood is our surrogate in this process of recognition and conversion.

Robert Brinkmeyer, in *The Art and Vision of Flannery O'Connor* (1989), also makes use of Bakhtin to rescue "the sacramental vision" (3) in O'Connor for real use in history. For Brinkmeyer, the "problem" is less aesthetic (being unwilling, as Gentry asserts, to see oneself as a grotesque in need of redemption) as it is sociopolitical: O'Connor's seeming heroes (Hazel Motes, for example) seem too "fundamentalist" and redneck to garner our support. According to Brinkmeyer, O'Connor rises above this problem in *Wise Blood* by shifting point of view from the omniscient to Mrs. Flood at the conclusion of the novel. In this volume of essays, Brinkmeyer continues the quest to reconcile O'Connor's sacramental vision with the demands of the secular.

"I never was one to go over the Civil War in a big way . . ."

Another topic that comes perennially into discussion of O'Connor is her Southernness. She packaged a couple of conference talks to settle the question, but that has not satisfied our appetite for the answer. A couple of points seem to surface over and over: Which does the most for her fiction, her Catholic faith or her regional identity? Who is trying to enlist her into the Southern ranks and what is at stake at the time? Did she actually mean all those snide things she said about the South in her letters?

When *Wise Blood* was first published, to be a Southern writer was to be a connoisseur of freaks and an addict of violence, the more bizarre the better. Caldwell, Capote, McCullers led the way; even Eudora Welty was viewed in the seamy light of Southern Gothic. Faulkner was in one critical forum a world-class American modernist of universal value; in another he was still the author of *Sanctuary*, the perpetrator of the infamous rape by corncob. John W. Aldridge, looking for trouble, attacked the young Southern literary establishment of the early 1950s, and O'Connor along with it, in an essay called "The Writer in the University." O'Connor was only one of several targets, many of them Southern writers. She was, in Aldridge's view, "decidedly minor," with one novel and one collection of short stories in print at the time (8). She was nothing more than a confection designed by a literary coterie for a specific market:

> [Flannery O'Connor] has lately become the official "younger Southern novelist" of the quarterlies. Her fiction has to do, in the main, with simple Southern peasant folk set against rustic Southern backgrounds, and for the academic Northern intellectual what is Southern and rustic is synonymous with all that is original, serious, and true in American letters. In a sense, Miss O'Connor does for the academic intellectuals what Truman Capote does for the pseudointellectuals of the flossy New York fashion-magazine world – she provides them with tone or chic, a little sprinkling of fake magnolia blossoms. . . . (59)

Louis D. Rubin, Jr., took up Aldridge's challenge in an reply published in the special issue of *Critique* mentioned previously. Rubin argued that there is substance where Aldridge sees only special-interest maneuvering. In fact, Rubin claims, the fiction is strongest when and where it leans least on religion and most on region. Rubin's O'Connor gets the social reality of the South that Caldwell fakes, but she also goes her senior one better by replacing his antiliterary "social consciousness" with a moral conscience.

Rubin has continued this line of interpretation for several decades now. In his view O'Connor's best work manifests the typically Southern view of human personal and social imperfectibility, the sense of evil and of the transcendent that mark the mind of the South, the sense of place from which all Southern writers draw their energy and vision. He ranks her just behind William Faulkner.

But it is dangerous to assume too much about O'Connor's allegiance to the South, through its community or through its literary traditions. She was often asked the question and had prepared formal comments by way of answers. It would be a mistake, for example, to fit O'Connor's work snugly within the traditional Southern ideology as the Agrarians have become identified with it. Melvin J. Friedman's introduction to *Critical Essays on Flannery O'Connor* (1985), for example, probably overestimates the evidence when he claims that O'Connor "is essentially an Agrarian sensibility, nurtured on such anti-industrial, anti-scientific texts as the 1930 *I'll Take My Stand*" (1). O'Connor, by her own account, did not read the Agrarian manifesto until 1964, the last year of her life, and knew at first look that, as a program for social and political action, it was "futile of course" (*HB* 566). In 1956 she wrote that she was pleased to see "the Agrarian business" applied to her own work (*HB* 148), but that is not the same as being "nurtured" on it. She was nurtured on New Criticism, and professed ignorance of the Southern ideological debates as a way of avoiding being dragged into them. It must be said, as well, that she had bought but not read the counter-Agrarian treatise, Cash's *The Mind of the South* (*HB* 225).

All of this is not to say that the conservative, traditional bent of the Agrarian position is not compatible with her own stands on several issues. It was. "The South in other words," she wrote to a young Southern writer in 1958, "still believes that man has fallen and that he is only perfectible by God's grace, not by his own

15

unaided efforts" (*HB* 302). It was this conservatism that, probably, prompted her to make what today we might consider insensitive and demeaning references to her black neighbors (*HB* 66), and to make her famous (or infamous) remark, in 1959: "I can't see James Baldwin in Georgia" (*HB* 329). It was, and is, a stumbling block for some readers of O'Connor, this apparent obliviousness to the racial turmoil through which she lived. Crews formulates the problem better, and more succinctly, than anyone else (157–60). But he gives O'Connor perhaps less credit for taking a stand than she deserves: she knew about Dr. Martin Luther King and his campaign for racial equality, she just preferred Cassius Clay's (later Muhammed Ali) stand on the matter (*HB* 580).

Being drawn into political and social controversies was one thing. Being conscripted into the party of Southern literature was another, about which O'Connor was perhaps less ambivalent. She tried to maintain a balance between being a Catholic writer and being a regional writer, with the weight of the balance on the side of religion. The forces of Southern literature were formidable. There was Faulkner looming over everyone who came after him like Michelangelo looming over the late Italian Renaissance. O'Connor was evasive: *Light in August* was "*I guess* a classic" (emphasis added). "I stay clear of Faulkner," she added, "so my own little boat won't get swamped" (*HB* 273). For more public consumption she called Faulkner "the Dixie *Limited*" (emphasis added).

She knew the myth of the Southern writer, as Faulkner had come to create and embody it, and she did not want to get so close as to be compared or judged by it. Instead, she peppered away at the myth, dodged comparison, and set sly charges in strategically chosen spots. One young male Southern writer piqued her attention as a "Southern Young Man of Parts" when he came to Milledgeville to do some research for fiction that apparently never materialized:

> [he] is busy building himself up to be Quentin [Compson]. I think they all want to go to Harvard or Princeton so they can sit in a window and say I hate it I hate it but I have to go back. Or maybe they only learn to say it after they get up there. (*HB* 63–4)

Not surprisingly, her own maneuverings have not stopped the critics from assessing her Southernness. Josephine Hendin, in *The*

World of Flannery O'Connor (1970), concludes that O'Connor and her competitor Capote "have abandoned the South's most distinctive concerns" (147), which Hendin lists as a concern for history, a living scale of personal and social values, an attachment to place. If O'Connor has any Southernness at all, in Hendin's view, it is negative Southernness: her entire body of work might be seen as an attempt to escape the imprisonment of the role of dutiful Southern daughter (13).

Miles Orvell's highly praised *Invisible Parade: The Fiction of Flannery O'Connor* (1972) also investigates the matter of the South in O'Connor's fiction, concluding: "Her concern was less with uncovering the tensions in race relations, less with the Southerner's adjustments to the modern world, than with uncovering the self-deceptions and evasions that keep us from recognizing our identities in a context rather larger than the immediately contemporary one" (10). Clearly, Orvell, with the majority of O'Connor's critics, prefers the "larger" ethical-moral setting to the more immediate social-historical one. The latter seems less rich in nuance than what he calls "a sense of the mystery of human life" (16).

Even as dedicated a sociologist as Robert Coles, in his *Flannery O'Connor's South* (1980), finds an O'Connor who dwelt in a moral world more complex and ultimately more meaningful than the segregated South of the 1950s and 1960s. The culmination of this reluctance, or refusal, to see O'Connor's work in its time is Marion Montgomery's *Why Flannery O'Connor Stayed Home* (1981), a densely argued book that braids philosophical temperament and overheated New Criticism into a whip with which to beat "the age" for its alleged obtuseness and gnostic reliance on humanist values. O'Connor, Montgomery informs us, was a fellow soldier in the losing battle against modernity, but she buried her polemic in metaphor (23).

> "If you don't like it ['Greenleaf'], don't fail to say so. I have a heart of pure steel."

The essays in this volume aim to pick up crosscurrents and dissent in the mainstream of O'Connor thinking, and to begin to build a countercurrent. It is time to deflect the main current if for no other reason than that it has incised a deep, narrow groove in our sense of O'Connor and her work, and we all stand in peril of being sucked into the vortex whether we want to leap or not. Crews, aware of the fixedness of critical thinking on O'Connor, tends to skepticism of "trendsetters" in the newer criticism. I do not; I believe that we and the fiction have much to gain by declaring a moratorium on the old ways.

"New" approaches to O'Connor's work, you would not be totally surprised to learn, are not so new. Some (the feminist, for example) have lain dormant in extant criticism, waiting for the moment to ripen. Others O'Connor herself waved off (Freudian psychoanalytic, for another example) and her partisans have continued the embargo. The dead hand of the New Criticism has gripped the interpreters of the fiction from its grave.

Josephine Hendin's earlier work (1970) seems to have been positioned in orthodox O'Connor studies as the creature of excess. Frederick Asals, for example, identifies his own "ferocious dissent" from Hendin's view as the "stimulus" for his own work, *Flannery O'Connor: The Imagination of Extremity* (1982). Hendin had located poles of tension within O'Connor's work, and had tacitly expanded the confines of the work to include some but not all of the conditions of the author's life situation: a Southerner, a woman, a daughter, a sufferer of "the slow violence of disease" (11). Hendin's case is made on the basis that the existential circumstances of O'Connor's life preceded and shaped the allegedly essential, the religious. Because of those circumstances, Flannery O'Connor was subject to "violent and destructive impulses" (16) that she could not direct against the original targets (herself, her mother, her society), and so turned upon surrogates in her fiction. Disease, Hendin argues, only drove the contradictions more deeply into O'Connor's psyche, making the eruptions more violent. Hendin, consequently, sees O'Connor's gallery of freaks, including Hazel Motes, not as figures for the unredeemed of mankind but as projections of the author's complex, conflicted self-image. The body in her fiction is an oppressor or trap; no good can come of it, or to it. From Hazel Motes on, her protagonists rage to escape the body or to defeat it; it is, Hendin claims, "a trap

more profound than . . . the power of Romans over Christians"
(39). Hendin sees O'Connor gravitating more and more closely
into an orbit with the Misfit: "the oppressed, the psychic cripple,
the freak – of all those who are martyred by silent fury and
redeemed through violence" (42).

The O'Connor mainstream still resists such reading of the life
into the work, although there have been some approaches. Dorothy Walters's foundational study (1973) admits the obvious, that
O'Connor's father's death from lupus and the daughter's own
illness constituted an "obvious source of a pervasive concern of
her writing: omnipresent death and disaster" (16). Walters, however, one step down the track, backs up, opting instead for a
generic key to the fiction.

Hendin's darker view of author and work is also detectable in
Martha Stephens's *The Question of Flannery O'Connor* (1973). The
"question" at issue is not the one posed overtly by O'Connor:
who shall be saved? How? Rather, the question is one that involves the reader and her response: How shall we take this view
of human nature and human life? "For what is oppressive about
the O'Connor work as a whole," Stephens asserts, "what is sometimes intolerable, is her stubborn refusal to see any good, any
beauty or dignity or meaning, in ordinary life on earth" (9).
Many of O'Connor's defenders find her morose view bracing, and
therefore consider Stephens's question banal. But, after decades
of indoctrination on *Wise Blood,* for example, it is useful to return
to a view of the novel as presenting "the most remorselessly
squalid picture of human life" (51). Stephens even goes so far as
to suggest that O'Connor burlesques herself in Sabbath Lily's
stories and her grotesque parody of motherhood in embracing the
musty mummy brought to her by Enoch. Stephens sees no relief:

> a feeling for the humanity of the characters that transcends ques-
> tions of conscious belief, a reaffirmation of his [the reader's] sense
> that there is a wide range of belief within which we can still
> respond to a character as a man or woman – is just exactly the
> kind of liberal feeling towards belief that O'Connor means to at-
> tack. . . . (74)

Stephens echoes, in her conclusion, the response of O'Connor's
friend John Hawkes, who argued in the *Sewanee Review* a decade

earlier that O'Connor seemed a little too fond of the demonic to claim to be a genuine Christian.

Stephens speculates that O'Connor's illness must have had a lot to do with the shape of her fiction, but she ultimately declines to guess which factors in the author's life might have led her from "normal" to "so fierce and forbidding a mode of fiction" (89, 95). A few years later, Carol Schloss, in *Flannery O'Connor's Dark Comedies* (1980), also broaches the topic of biographical sources for fiction, but also declines to make anything like a conclusion (6–7).

The record of O'Connor criticism in essays rather than in books and monographs is somewhat more full of un- or antiorthodox views. Claire Kahane's "Flannery O'Connor's Rage of Vision" (1974) proposes to locate and name "at the center of [her] work . . . a psychological demand which overshadows her religious intent, shaping plot, image and character as well as her distinctive narrative voice" (121). This deeply embedded source of energy and shaping power is the parent–child encounter, about which O'Connor was, Kahane implies, strongly ambivalent:

> There is, then, a sadistic quality to the [O'Connor] narrator, who acts as an archaic superego, a primitive internalized image of the parent forcing the characters through the triadic ritual of sin, humiliation and redemption by wit as well as by plot structure. (121)

More recently James Mellard has argued that Lacanian psychoanalytic methods provide better insight into the fiction than the tried and true religious metaphors. More traditionalist critics object, as does Crews (147–9), to what they see as an arbitrary and subversive substitution for the author's often-stated intent. But holders of this position too quickly forget that O'Connor was far from being a naive reader of Freud (Lacan's predecessor); she could be quite cagey in her own manipulations of the Freudian vocabulary (see her story "The Comforts of Home"). She wrote to "A":

> As to Sigmund, I am against him tooth and toenail but crafty: never deny, seldom confirm, always distinguish. Within his limitations I am ready to admit certain uses for him. (*HB* 110)

There is always a level of self-conscious parody and deflection in O'Connor's fiction, Mellard argues, and the Lacanian approach, which he extends in the present essay, is the best way to see O'Connor fiction whole and steady.

Theoretical approaches to O'Connor have also, recently, moved in the direction of gender. Whether O'Connor would have made a feminist is an open question; her statements on and about the matter are not conclusive. She was, for instance, well aware of the gender bias historically upheld in the Catholic Church, yet she seemed to prefer to blame the individual male "So&So" rather than the structure of the religion (*HB* 168). Hendin's early and later work (1970 and 1978) proposes an O'Connor deeply motivated by a desire to escape the trap of the Southern daughter syndrome. And a more antique form of feminism was claimed by Martha Stephens, who saw O'Connor as a short story writer by fiat of gender, a novelist reluctantly:

> She would have despaired at the very idea of attempting the complicated, sprawling, abundant novel that her southern male compatriots were writing – Wolfe, somewhat before her time of course, Faulkner, Styron, and Warren. Nothing was more foreign to her than that; and like many women writers, her impulse, one feels, when she confronted such works must have been to pitch in and clear them out and straighten them up. (44)

The genuine, sound feminist reading has had to wait for Louise Westling in *Sacred Groves and Ravaged Gardens* (1985); in this work a feminist perspective turned upon O'Connor's work finds its counterpart in the fiction. Skillfully weaving O'Connor's letters, essays, and fiction, Westling places O'Connor persuasively within a tradition of woman's writing that includes her immediate Southern sisters (Welty and McCullers) and the longer tradition of writing by women.

As you might gather from most of the preceding discussion, the historical context of O'Connor's work has been the least-explored critical territory. If your premise is that O'Connor quite rightly sought to rise above her "here-and-now" for religious reasons, then the here-and-now becomes irrelevant without argument. But O'Connor was not oblivious to the world around her; in fact she confessed quite early to an addiction to "a few sideline researches into the ways of the vulgar" (*HB* 49). To her the vulgar included everything from stories of Roy Rogers's horse in church to political gossip and the movies of W. C. Fields. In other words, it would be a mistake to read her work as if all it had to offer was single-channel communication with the Omnipotent. Lance Bacon's essay in this volume, a taste of his book on O'Connor, is the first substantial critical work to restore O'Connor to the full, rich context of her time and place.

"Sit at yr. machine"

From O'Connor's point of view her writing was vastly simpler than the constructions we critics have made or professed to have found in it. "I am a pretty insensitive soul for subtleties," she once wrote, perhaps disingenuously, "and so forth but then one never writes for a subtle reader" (*HB* 296). But the state of our critical understanding of any O'Connor story, *Wise Blood* included, begins on a level of subtlety that has been in part created by the flourishing industry in O'Connor studies. Perhaps you have had coffee in one of her mugs, or seen John Huston's film of *Wise Blood,* or read the novel in a reading group.

In this general introduction to the four new essays in criticism that follow, my purpose has been to outline the "old" ways of critical thinking and to persuade you to read (or reread) *Wise Blood* with the "new" in mind. We never come upon literature without preparation, even though often that preparation is unknown to us. At a certain moment in the history of reading certain works, the accumulated "understanding" of the text outpaces the text. We have arrived at such a moment in the reading of *Wise Blood.* We can't go back to the beginning. I've tried to warn you about the history of reading *Wise Blood,* with the hope that the information might make your reading of the novel more interesting if it can no longer be (if it ever could have been) unmediated.

WORKS CITED

Aladjim, Henrietta. *Understanding Lupus.* New York: Charles Scribners Sons, 1982.
Aldridge, John W. "The Writer in the University." *In Search of Heresy:*

American Literature in an Age of Conformity. 1956; rpt. Port Washington, N.Y.: Kennikat Press, 1967. 35–69.

Asals, Frederick. *Flannery O'Connor: The Imagination of Extremity.* Athens: University of Georgia Press, 1982.

Brinkmeyer, Robert. *The Art and Vision of Flannery O'Connor.* Baton Rouge: Louisiana State University Press, 1989.

Brooks, Cleanth, and Robert Penn Warren. *Understanding Fiction.* New York: F. S. Crofts and Company, 1943. (This is the first edition; there were many subsequent editions O'Connor might have used.)

Browning, Preston M., Jr. *Flannery O'Connor.* Carbondale: Southern Illinois University Press, 1974.

Cash, W. J. *The Mind of the South.* New York: Alfred A. Knopf, 1941.

Coles, Robert. *Flannery O'Connor's South.* Baton Rouge: Louisiana State University Press, 1980.

Crews, Frederick. *The Critics Bear It Away: American Fiction and the Academy.* New York: Random House, 1992.

Desmond, John F. *Risen Sons: Flannery O'Connor's Vision of History.* Athens: University of Georgia Press, 1987.

Drake, Robert. *Flannery O'Connor: A Critical Essay.* [Grand Rapids, Mich.]: William P. Eerdmans, 1966.

Feeley, Kathleen, S.S.N.D. *Flannery O'Connor: Voice of the Peacock.* New Brunswick, N.J.: Rutgers University Press, 1972. Foreword by Caroline Gordon.

Friedman, Melvin J., and Beverly Lyon Clark, eds. *Critical Essays on Flannery O'Connor.* Boston: G. K. Hall, 1985.

Gentry, Marshall Bruce. *Flannery O'Connor's Religion of the Grotesque.* Jackson: University Press of Mississippi, 1986.

Gordon, Caroline. "Flannery O'Connor's *Wise Blood.*" *Critique* II (Fall 1958): 3–10.

Gordon, Caroline, and Allen Tate. *The House of Fiction.* New York: Charles Scribner's Sons, 1950. (A second edition, published in 1960, included a short story by O'Connor.)

Gossett, Louise Y. "Flannery O'Connor." In Louis D. Rubin, Jr., et al., eds., *The History of Southern Literature.* Baton Rouge: Louisiana State University Press, 1985. 89–93.

Hawkes, John. "Flannery O'Connor's Devil." *Sewanee Review* 70 (1962), 395–407. Rpt. in Friedman and Clark.

Hendin, Josephine. *The World of Flannery O'Connor.* Bloomington: Indiana University Press, 1970.

Vulnerable People: A View of American Fiction since 1945. New York: Oxford University Press, 1978.

Hyman, Stanley Edgar. *Flannery O'Connor.* Minneapolis: University of Minnesota Press, 1966.

Kahane, Claire. "Flannery O'Connor's Rage of Vision." *American Literature* 46 (Winter 1974): 54–67. Rpt. in Friedman and Clark.

LaFarge, Oliver. "Manic Gloom." *Saturday Review,* May 17, 1952, 22.

Lewis, R. W. B. "Eccentrics' Pilgrimage." *Hudson Review* VI (Spring 1953): 144–50.

May, John R. *The Pruning Word: The Parables of Flannery O'Connor.* Notre Dame, Ind.: University of Notre Dame Press, 1976.

Mellard, James M. "Flannery O'Connor's *Others:* Freud, Lacan, and the Unconscious." *American Literature* 61 (December 1989): 624–43.

Montgomery, Marion. *Why Flannery O'Connor Stayed Home.* Chicago: Sherwood Sugden, 1981.

O'Connor, Flannery. *The Habit of Being.* Ed. Sally Fitzgerald. New York: Random House, 1979.

　Wise Blood. 1952; rpt. New York: Farrar, Straus & Giroux, 1962.

Orvell, Miles. *Invisible Parade: The Fiction of Flannery O'Connor.* Philadelphia: Temple University Press, 1972. (See also the reissue of Orvell's book: *Flannery O'Connor: An Introduction.* Jackson: University Press of Mississippi, 1991. Orvell's preface to the latter book is particularly interesting as the testimony of a critic who has been in O'Connor studies for two decades and weathered many attacks.)

Rosenfeld, Isaac. "To Win by Default." *New Republic,* July 7, 1952, 19–20.

Rubin, Louis D., Jr. Review of *A Good Man Is Hard To Find* by Flannery O'Connor. *Sewanee Review* 63 (1955): 671–81. Rpt. in Friedman and Clark.

　"Flannery O'Connor: A Note on Literary Fashions." *Critique* II (Fall 1958): 11–18.

Schloss, Carol. *Flannery O'Connor's Dark Comedies: The Limits of Inference.* Baton Rouge: Louisiana State University Press, 1980.

Schur, Peter H., M.D., ed. *The Clinical Management of Systemic Lupus Erythematosus.* New York: Grune & Stratton, 1983.

Simons, John W. "A Case of Possession." *Commonweal* 56 (June 27, 1952): 297–8.

Stephens, Martha. *The Question of Flannery O'Connor.* Baton Rouge: Louisiana State University Press, 1973.

Towers, Robert. "Flannery O'Connor's Gifts." *New York Review of Books,* May 3, 1979, 3–6.

Twelve Southerners. *I'll Take My Stand.* New York: Harper & Brothers, 1930.

Walters, Dorothy. *Flannery O'Connor.* New York: Twayne, 1973.

Westling, Louise. *Sacred Groves and Ravaged Gardens: The Fiction of Eudora Welty, Carson McCullers, and Flannery O'Connor.* Athens: University of Georgia Press, 1985.

A Fondness for Supermarkets: *Wise Blood* and Consumer Culture

JON LANCE BACON

IN 1951 an analyst of American popular culture described a woman whose legs could be detached for sales purposes. "The Mechanical Bride," as Marshall McLuhan called her, appeared in an advertisement for Gotham Hosiery. More precisely, her legs appeared by themselves in the advertisement, which placed the limbs "on a Pedestal." McLuhan criticized this sort of commercial imagery because it encouraged "that strange dissociation of sex not only from the human person but even from the unity of the body." Ultimately, this sales technique had diminished the self-hood of the target audience:

> To the mind of the modern girl, legs, like busts, are power points which she has been taught to tailor, but as parts of the success kit rather than erotically or sensuously. . . . As such, her legs are not intimately associated with her taste or with her unique self but are merely display objects like the grill work on a car.

In short, "the smartly turned-out girl walks and behaves like a being who *sees* herself as a slick object rather than is aware of herself as a person" (McLuhan 98, 99).

In 1955 one of McLuhan's readers created a female character with a detachable leg. The portrayal of Joy-Hulga in the short story, "Good Country People," reveals a strong affinity between Flannery O'Connor and the author of "The Mechanical Bride," which O'Connor advised a friend to read "completely and slowly" (*The Habit of Being* [*HB*] 173). Like McLuhan's "modern girl," who uses her legs as "date-baited power levers for the management of the male audience" (98), Joy-Hulga knows that her wooden leg impresses the Bible salesman she plans to seduce. Like McLuhan, O'Connor relates the imagery of body parts to the idea of selfhood. The "modern girl" and Joy-Hulga seem to be opposites in this respect; Joy-Hulga takes care of her artificial leg "as someone else would his soul," and she feels that the salesman has "touched the truth about her" when he observes that the leg is "what makes you different. You ain't like anybody else" (*The Complete Stories* [*CS*] 288, 289). When Manley Pointer steals her leg, however, she succumbs to the "cultural dynamics" identified by McLuhan – the dynamics of "replaceable parts" (98). Manipulated by a salesman, Joy-Hulga loses her sense of self. The loss may be a blessing in disguise, if it forces her to seek an identity based on something other than "Nothing" (*CS* 277), but the salesman is hardly motivated by a desire to increase her self-awareness. To him, Joy-Hulga is just another victim. "One time I got a woman's glass eye this way," he boasts (*CS* 291). Like the advertisers criticized in *The Mechanical Bride*, Pointer has made a career of reducing women to body parts.

The triumph of the salesman, and the damage to selfhood, concerned O'Connor deeply. Indeed, the figure of the salesman makes frequent appearances in the fiction she produced from the late 1940s to the early 1960s. The husband of the protagonist in "A Stroke of Good Fortune" (1949) sells Miracle Products. The protagonist in "Greenleaf" (1956) has a son who sells insurance; one of the main characters from *The Violent Bear It Away* ([*VBA*] 1960) has a father in the same line. The father, who calls himself "a prophet of life insurance" (*VBA* 59), is not the only salesman in the novel. A manufacturer's representative also shows up, selling Southern Copper Parts and dispensing professional advice. He claims, for instance, that "you couldn't sell a copper flue to a man you didn't love," since "love was the only policy that worked 95% of the time" (*VBA* 50, 51).

A profession guided by the philosophy of the copper flue salesman would seem to repel any thoughtful person, but even aspiring intellectuals take sales jobs in O'Connor's fiction. The protagonists of two stories from 1961 find themselves in this situation: Julian sells typewriters in "Everything That Rises Must Converge," while Calhoun sells air conditioners, boats, and refrigerators in "The Partridge Festival." For each character, salesmanship means the deferment of true selfhood. Julian would rather be a writer, and Calhoun works as a salesman during the summer months "so that for the other nine months he could afford to meet life naturally and bring his real self – the rebel-artist-mystic – to birth" (*CS* 424). Calhoun, in particular, understands the connection between sales and individual identity. During the summer, "the orgy of selling" completely transforms his personality. "In the face of a customer," O'Connor writes, "he was carried outside himself . . ." (*The Complete Stories* [*CS*] 425).

The relation between salesmanship and selfhood receives its fullest treatment in the novel O'Connor published one year after McLuhan published *The Mechanical Bride*. In *Wise Blood* ([*WB*] 1952), O'Connor depicts a society pervaded by advertising and marketing techniques. Her depiction is satirical, and the target of her satire is much larger than the urban South, which provides the setting for the novel. *Wise Blood* represents her critique of American consumer culture, whose period of greatest expansion coincided with her literary career. One of her essays, "The Fiction Writer and His Country" (1957), illustrates this coincidence. Responding to a 1955 editorial in *Life* magazine, O'Connor rejected the idea that the "unparalleled prosperity" of the United States in the decade following World War II compelled American novelists to write fiction "that really represented this country . . ." (*Mystery and Manners* [*MM*] 25–6). O'Connor left such "affirmative" gestures to the advertising agencies (*MM* 34). In *Wise Blood*, she inverts the meaning then attached to material prosperity. The signs of consumer society that appear throughout the novel hardly justify national celebration. They suggest, instead, the growing power of the advertisers – the increasing influence that corporate capitalism would exert over individual identity.[1]

When she discussed consumerism with interviewers, O'Connor tended to emphasize its detrimental effect on regional identity. In a 1959 interview she maintained that Southerners were losing their "regional sense" primarily "because everybody wants the good things of life, like supermarkets . . ." (qtd. in Hoy and Sullivan 30). O'Connor has long been recognized as a defender of Southern identity and a recorder of the "fading manners" that had distinguished the South from "the rest of the country" (*MM*

29). But her regional loyalty has distracted readers from her participation in a nationwide debate regarding the status of individualism under corporate capitalism. Southerners were not the only Americans who feared a nationally homogeneous culture, or who feared for the survival of individuality in such a culture. The defenders of Southern identity shared these concerns with social observers like David Riesman, author of *The Lonely Crowd* (1950), and William H. Whyte, author of *The Organization Man* (1956). To this extent O'Connor fell in line with other American intellectuals after World War II. Her fiction reflects the widespread tendency to perceive conformity as a defining characteristic of postwar America.[2]

The social paradigm with the greatest intellectual currency, during the 1950s, tied conformity to mass consumption. The paradigm encouraged hyperbole on the part of American intellectuals, to whom the Soviet Union represented mass society at its worst. In a 1952 symposium published by *Partisan Review*, Louis Kronenberger treated Soviet totalitarianism and American "mass culture" as parallel threats to individuality. He wrote, "In the exact same way that we oppose regimentation of thought on political grounds, we must oppose regimentation of taste on cultural ones." The symposium editors blamed mass culture for the problems encountered by the group that upheld "the tradition of critical non-conformism" in America: "the intellectual minority." In fact, the editors hoped that the symposium would yield an appropriate intellectual response to mass culture. They asked the contributors: "Must the American intellectual and writer adapt himself to mass culture?" Newton Arvin spoke for most of the respondents when he urged intellectuals "to master and to fertilize it" ("Our Country" 285, 286, 287, 445).

In *The Mechanical Bride*, McLuhan proposed another strategy for dealing with consumer culture, "a method for reversing the process" by which "commercial education" brought about "public helplessness." In short, McLuhan analyzed the very advertising that was supposed to "keep everybody in the helpless state." He asked, "Why not use the new commercial education as a means to enlightening its intended prey? Why not assist the public to observe consciously the drama which is intended to operate upon it unconsciously?" Like Kronenberger, McLuhan thought that mass consumption threatened individuality. "When men and women . . . have become accustomed to the consumption of uniform products," McLuhan wrote, "it is hard to see where any individualism remains" (v, 55).

O'Connor expresses the same anxiety in *Wise Blood,* inundating her characters with commercial appeals. Electric signs that "moved up and down or blinked frantically" define the boundaries of the urban setting, Taulkinham; the signs for "PEANUTS, WESTERN UNION, AJAX, TAXI, HOTEL, CANDY" inform Hazel Motes that he has reached the city (*WB* 29). The window displays in the downtown business district captivate shoppers: "No one was paying any attention to the sky. The stores in Taulkinham stayed open on Thursday nights so that people could have an extra opportunity to see what was for sale" (*WB* 37). In this commercial setting, the man who sells potato peelers has built an "altar" to his product, a pyramid of green cardboard boxes atop a card table (*WB* 38). When Hazel visits the city park in which Enoch Emery works, Enoch takes him to a hot dog stand whose very structure advertises a product. The FROSTY BOTTLE is "in the shape of an Orange Crush with frost painted in blue around the top of it" (*WB* 82). Inside the stand, "there was a large advertisement for ice cream, showing a cow dressed up like a housewife" (*WB* 88). Even the rural countryside, which Enoch and Hazel have left for the city, contains advertising messages. "CCC snuff ads" are pasted on deserted farm buildings (*WB* 12–13, 207).

Beyond their scenic function, the techniques of advertising and marketing featured in the novel have significance for individual identity. O'Connor first suggests this by placing Enoch in front of a product display that dwarfs him. She sets Enoch against a Walgreen's window, "against a background of alarm clocks, toilet waters, candies, sanitary pads, fountain pens, and pocket flashlights, displayed in all colors to twice his height" (*WB* 135). Enoch is the character most closely identified with consumerism, the character whose "fondness for Supermarkets" leads him "to spend an hour or so in one every afternoon . . . browsing around among the canned goods and reading the cereal stories" (*WB*

130). At home he spends time looking at the commercial illustrations that hang on his walls: "They were over calendars and had been sent him by the Hilltop Funeral Home and the American Rubber Tire Company" (*WB* 133).

As a consumer Enoch exemplifies the "public helplessness" that McLuhan hoped to remedy by analyzing advertising. Enoch is pathetically vulnerable to advertising messages. Outside a movie theater, he sees "a large illustration of a monster stuffing a young woman into an incinerator." He cannot fight the impulse to watch something he is afraid to watch:

> I ain't going in no picture show like that, he said, giving it a nervous look. I'm going home. I ain't going to wait around in no picture show. I ain't got the money to buy a ticket, he said, taking out his purse again. I ain't even going to count thisyer change.
> It ain't but forty-three cent here, he said, that ain't enough. A sign said the price of a ticket for adults was forty-five cents, balcony, thirty-five. I ain't going to sit in no balcony, he said, buying a thirty-five cent ticket.
> I ain't going in, he said.
> Two doors flew open and he found himself moving down a long red foyer and then up a darker tunnel and then up a higher, still darker tunnel. (*WB* 138)

Enoch ends up watching a triple feature. He might blame his "wise blood" for making him act against his will, but the movie poster is the immediate impetus. Clearly, Enoch is motivated by an internal compulsion he does not understand. He feels he is "always having to do something that something else wanted him to do," and this inner drive places even his purchases beyond his control; since the "new jesus" requires a "tabernacle," Enoch has "to spend all his money on drapes and gilt" for its decoration (*WB* 135, 137, 174, 175). At the same time, however, the external stimulus of advertising determines the particular manner in which his internal compulsion will be expressed.[3]

In the twelfth chapter of the novel, Enoch experiences an "awakening" (*WB* 194). He suddenly understands how he will be "rewarded" for following the dictates of his blood (*WB* 191), and his recompense, he thinks, will involve an advertising gimmick. "I know what I want," Enoch murmurs after reading a newspaper advertisement for a movie and its star, "Gonga, Giant Jungle

Monarch," whose publicity tour of local theaters will end that evening at the Victory on 57th Street (*WB* 193, 194). The promotional tour consists of a man in an apesuit shaking hands with moviegoers. Impressed by the example of Gonga, who can attract a crowd of young fans, Enoch longs for the same kind of public attention: "He wanted, some day, to see a line of people waiting to shake his hand" (*WB* 191).

Enoch hopes to realize the promise conveyed by the advertising he has seen, the promise of personal distinction. He aspires "to be THE young man of the future, like the ones in the insurance ads" (*WB* 191). The statement yokes together contradictory desires: to stand out, to fit in. It is the contradiction that McLuhan located at "the center of the drama of a consumer economy." In this drama, the individual was "torn between the fear of being a misfit and the passion for the distinction conferred by purchasing a mass-produced item." In *The Mechanical Bride*, McLuhan analyzed an advertisement implying that men who consume Lord Calvert Whiskey "are distinct from the herd." McLuhan intended for his readers to reject "the notion of distinction and culture as being a matter of consumption rather than the possession of discriminating perception and judgment" (48, 58). Enoch misses the irony to which McLuhan directed attention – the irony of basing personal distinction on the commercial imagery used to promote consumption. By appropriating that imagery, Enoch believes, he can emerge "as an entirely new man, with an even better personality than he had now" (*WB* 175). Specifically, Enoch hopes to gain distinction by stealing the promotional gimmick, the apesuit, and wearing it himself.

Helpless to resist the appeal of a movie poster, he is likewise vulnerable to the ways in which advertising validates personal identity or withholds validation. Enoch will change "the way I am" to fit the model of individual distinction that he has seen in front of the movie theater: "a successful ape" shaking the hands of his fans (*WB* 178, 194). This role model has suggested that Enoch's own identity, grounded in his own experience, is unimportant. Enoch greets Gonga by identifying himself and recounting the facts of his life. "My name is Enoch Emery," he says. "I attended the Rodemill Boys' Bible Academy. I work at the city zoo. . . . I'm only eighteen year old but I already work for the city." Gonga responds by humiliating the young man who has seen two of the movies in the Gonga series. "The star" tells the movie consumer to "go to hell" (*WB* 182).

Impelled by the "envy" he feels when he watches other movie-goers line up to meet Gonga (*WB* 195), Enoch overpowers the man in the apesuit. Then, "burning with the intensest kind of happiness," he digs a hole and buries his clothes; the narrator suggests an analogy with "burying his former self" (*WB* 196). Donning the apesuit, Enoch anticipates a new and improved self. The narrative, however, shows only the loss of individual identity. Enoch will be obscured, not improved, by the commercial image. He disappears, leg by leg, arm by arm, into the apesuit: "A black heavier shaggier figure replaced his." The narrative no longer refers to Enoch by name. He becomes a two-headed, then a one-headed "it" (*WB* 197).

The appropriation of commercial imagery does not bring Enoch the distinction he expects. Dressed as Gonga, he extends his hand to a man and a woman. They do not shake his hand; instead, they flee from the "hideous" gorilla (*WB* 198). Critical readings of this scene usually interpret Enoch's transformation as a descent from the human into the bestial – an illustration of O'Connor's "grotesque" diminution of human stature (Allen 259–60, 268; Burns 160–1). But his transformation into a gorilla has less to do with animal nature than with consumer culture. In *Wise Blood,* forms of advertising and marketing envelop the self, submerging it in a world of salable objects. The scene that takes place at the Walgreen's drugstore foreshadows Enoch's submersion in the commercial image of Gonga. O'Connor describes a young woman who has become an inextricable element of a commercial display:

> The fountain counter was pink and green marble linoleum and behind it there was a red-headed waitress in a lime-colored uniform and a pink apron. She had green eyes set in pink and they resembled a picture behind her of a Lime-Cherry Surprise, a special that day for ten cents. (*WB* 136)

The description suggests more than the suppression of personality within the commercial setting. The waitress can take off the uniform and the apron after work, but her eyes will remain green and pink. Her identity has been assimilated into the presentation of the product, the fountain drink she pushes so aggressively: "Enoch couldn't decide which of several concoctions was the one for him to have until she ended it by moving one arm under the counter and bringing out a Lime-Cherry Surprise." When Enoch ignores her, she prepares a second Surprise and tries to force that on him (*WB* 137).

The idea that a salesperson would have to identify herself with the product being sold found expression in the contemporary critique of consumerism. C. Wright Mills explored the idea in *White Collar*, a sociological study published a year before *Wise Blood*. Mills noted the rise of a "personality market," in which the "personal or even intimate traits of the employee are drawn into the sphere of exchange and become of commercial relevance." These traits, he added, "become commodities in the labor market" (182). The situation of the waitress in *Wise Blood* is analogous, then, to the situation of a salesgirl described by Mills:

> The one area of her occupational life in which she might be "free to act," the area of her own personality, must now also be managed, must become the alert yet obsequious instrument by which goods are distributed.
>
> In the normal course of her work, because her personality becomes the instrument of an alien purpose, the salesgirl becomes self-alienated. (184)

The waitress with the eyes of green and pink appears only briefly in *Wise Blood*. Solace Layfield is the more prominent figure of self-alienation in the novel. The sales strategy most important to the plot is his impersonation of Hazel Motes. After Hazel refuses to work with Hoover Shoats and turn the Church Without Christ into a moneymaking venture, Hoover hires Solace and turns him into a sales instrument. Submerging his identity in that of Hazel, Solace becomes an "illusion." Solace, like Hazel, wears a "glare-blue" suit and a white hat; "the other Prophet," like the original, preaches from the hood of a "rat-colored" car (*WB* 166, 167, 204). The submersion of identity is not just a matter of physical appearance. In pretending to be Hazel, Solace has to deny his own Christian faith. Hazel recognizes that Solace is not being "true" to himself: "What do you get up on top of a car and say you don't believe in what you do believe in for?" (*WB* 203).

If Solace "ain't true," he also "mocks what is" (*WB* 204). Hazel suffers his own episode of self-alienation when he first sees Solace: "He had never pictured himself that way before." In effect, Hazel's identity is submerged in Hoover's reconception of "the True Prophet" (*WB* 167). Hazel regains his sense of self by forcing Solace to undress and by hitting the imposter with the rat-colored Essex: "The man didn't look so much like Haze, lying on the ground on his face without his hat or suit on" (*WB* 204).

Hazel uses his car to kill his impersonator, but the value he places on the Essex shows that Hazel himself has succumbed to a way of thinking fostered by consumer society. He links his identity with a product of American industry, a car "that ain't been built by a bunch of foreigners" (*WB* 126). As a place that Hazel "can always get away in," the Essex seems to confirm his self-conception as a totally free individual.[4] Praising his Essex, Hazel claims that "I knew when I first saw it that it was the car for me" (*WB* 115). His assertion resembles a promise made in advertising copy for Buick: "It makes you feel like the man you are." The author of a widely read study of advertising cited this copy to show how Madison Avenue encouraged consumers to view car ownership as a mode of self-expression. In *The Hidden Persuaders* (1957), Vance Packard observed that "American consumers were becoming self-image buyers." Drawing on the findings of motivational research, merchandisers had found it lucrative to "help people buy a projection of themselves." Packard conjectured that "the most spectacularly successful image building has been done by the automobile industry" (49, 52). Indeed, a study commissioned by the *Chicago Tribune* reported that Americans valued automobiles because they "provide avenues for the expression . . . of the character, temperament and self concept of the owner and driver" (qtd. in Packard 52–3).

O'Connor suggests that consumer society reneges on the advertised promise of self-expression. Consumers who identify themselves with products, or with the imagery used to advertise these products, will be disappointed and betrayed in their search for self-realization. As the image of Gonga fails to bring Enoch the distinction he desires, so the Essex fails Hazel. The car falls to pieces after a highway patrolman pushes it down a hill. The destruction of the product with which he has identified himself forces Hazel to consider the possibility of some reality other than the material. As Hazel looks out over the pasture in which his wrecked car lies, his face seems "to reflect the entire distance across the clearing and on beyond, the entire distance that extended from his eyes to the blank gray sky that went on, depth after depth, into space" (*WB* 209). The new worldview implicit in the description of a face "concentrated on space" (*WB* 210) has a fairly short duration within the novel. Hazel gains his new perspective in the penultimate chapter; in the final chapter, he dies. For the most part, materialism defines the existence of Hazel and the other characters. Their lives are circumscribed by the material world, understood in two ways – as a world in which the spiritual has no place, as a world in which everything is for sale.

The world of *Wise Blood* resembles "the new society" that Mills described in *White Collar*, the society in which "selling is a pervasive activity, unlimited in scope and ruthless in its choice of technique and manner." To postwar Americans, Mills wrote, salesmanship represented the social norm:

> The salesman's world has now become everybody's world, and, in some part, everybody has become a salesman. . . . The market now reaches into every institution and every relation. The bargaining manner, the huckstering animus, the memorized theology of pep, the commercialized evaluation of personal traits – they are all around us; in public and in private there is the tang and feel of salesmanship. (161)

In her novel O'Connor makes the social norm decidedly offensive. The harshness of her critique shows that O'Connor held a minority position, within the very ranks of "the intellectual minority," on the subject of mass consumption. She told a correspondent in 1959 that "some revolt against our exaggerated materialism is long overdue" (*HB* 336). For the majority of intellectuals, by contrast, the object of criticism was not materialism per se. After all, the nation was engaged in a Cold War, and material prosperity was supposed to show the superiority of American capitalism to Soviet communism. When Kronenberger drew his analogy between "regimentation of thought" and "regimentation of taste" in the *Partisan Review* symposium, he made it clear that he considered the first a foreign development, the second a domestic one. In other words the problems arising from *within* American society were aesthetic not ideological. Most contemporary intellectuals made the same distinction. Preferring the topic that was safer politically, the bogeyman of homogenized "taste," they neglected to criticize the modes of collective "thought" enforced by American consumer society.

To O'Connor, taste was a superficial concern. Her position was closer to that of Mills, a dissenting voice in the *Partisan Review* symposium, and to that of McLuhan. In *White Collar,* Mills criticized not merely the "style of life," but the very "ideology" of "a society that has turned itself into a fabulous salesroom" (165–6). In *The Mechanical Bride,* McLuhan tried to untie the "mental strait jackets" employed by consumer culture (58). While other intellectuals contended that their task should be to educate the taste of American consumers (Lears 45–6), O'Connor, Mills, and McLuhan expressed a desire to resist a consumerist ideology that dovetailed with the reigning political consensus.

Lamenting a culture in which "the capital of individual resistance and autonomous existence is being used up at a very visible rate," McLuhan suggested that "we would do well to strengthen those inner resources, which we still undoubtedly exert, to resist the mechanism of mass delirium and collective irrationalism." From his perspective, would-be resisters faced two problems: the combined power of the institutions they challenged, and a weak understanding of the form their challenge should take. McLuhan pointed to "the increasingly numerous mechanisms for anticipating and controlling the thoughts and feelings of many millions." Resisters were up against "the unofficial nationwide agencies of education, production, distribution, entertainment, and advertisement." To overcome the odds, resisters needed a clear strategy. Without "workable standards of securely civilized judgment," their challenge could prove ineffectual. Unfortunately, McLuhan remarked, "there are no accepted standards of submission or resistance to commercially sponsored appeals" (144). Resistance to consumer society seemed a rather vague proposition.

The question of strategy vexed O'Connor. One possibility was resistance organized along regional lines. Before World War II, the Agrarians had united "to support a Southern way of life against . . . the American or prevailing way" (Twelve Southerners ix). This example of organized regional opposition, circa 1930, did not impress O'Connor. Although she sympathized with the Agrarians, she felt their challenge to industrialism had been doomed to failure. When O'Connor read *I'll Take My Stand* for the first time, she considered it "interesting" but "futile of course." She likened the social and economic manifesto to a quaint poetic injunction: "Woodman, spare that tree" (*HB* 566).

If Southerners could not prevent social and economic change, Southern artists, at least, could organize to preserve regional distinctiveness in the realm of culture. In "The Regional Writer," a 1962 lecture, O'Connor mentioned one form of cultural organization: "Today, every self-respecting Southern college has itself an arts festival where Southern writers can be heard and where they are actually read and commented upon. . . ." Despite her participation in such events, she did not place much faith in the organized efforts of the Southern literary community. "All this sounds fine," she said in her lecture, "but while it has been happening, other ground has been shifting under our feet." Efforts to preserve and promote regional culture ran up against the homogenizing power of the national media, especially the medium of television. Evaluating the stories she had read at the 1957 Southern Writers' Conference, O'Connor complained that they had been influenced "only by the television" (*MM* 56). She expanded on this point in her correspondence, blaming television for displacing a regional idiom from Southern fiction. Participants in the conference had produced "television stories written in television language for the television world. The old souls don't know the South exists" (*HB* 234). O'Connor elsewhere disparaged the conference held in Athens, Georgia, for being "about as Southern as the southern part of Madison Avenue" (*The Correspondence of Flannery O'Connor and the Brainerd Cheneys* [C] 59). If Southern writers were "anguished" over the prospect of a South "more and more like the rest of the country" (*MM* 28–9), their writing itself was threatened by the language of television and advertising.[5]

O'Connor saw her own writing distorted by the conventions of television. She had misgivings about the sale of the television rights to her short story, "The Life You Save May Be Your Own" (1953). After she sold the rights in 1956, O'Connor predicted that the producers would add a happy ending, an ending that would include a plug for one of the network sponsors: "Mr. Shiftlet and the idiot daughter will no doubt go off in a Chrysler and live happily ever after" (*HB* 174). The producers did not, in fact, "make a musical out of it" (*HB* 186), but the version of the story broadcast on CBS did feature a musical film star, Gene Kelly, as Tom T. Shiftlet. Publicity regarding the 1957 *Schlitz Playhouse* adaptation suggested that it owed more to Hollywood versions of Southern life than to the narrative by O'Connor. In her correspondence, she quoted an announcement describing it as a "backwoods love story" and a statement by Kelly himself, who said, "It's a kind of hillbilly thing in which I play a guy who *befriends* a deaf-mute girl in the hills of Kentucky" (*HB* 191). O'Connor added the emphasis to indicate the discrepancy she saw between her story and the adaptation. "I didn't recognize the television version," she told an interviewer in 1962. The producers did as she had predicted: "they changed the ending just a bit by having Shiftlet suddenly get a conscience and come back for the girl" (qtd. in Wells 90).

O'Connor felt that any regional resistance to the national consumer culture would be ambivalent at best. Southerners themselves seemed to favor assimilation with the rest of the country. In a lecture from 1963, "The Catholic Novelist in the Protestant South," O'Connor noted a contradiction between "the South's instinct to preserve her identity" and "her equal instinct to fall eager victim to every poisonous breath from Hollywood or Madison Avenue" (*MM* 200). The attraction of consumer goods seemed overwhelming.

In her religion O'Connor found a less ambivalent response to consumer culture. As a Catholic novelist she embraced not only a religious position, but also an economic perspective. "Certainly," she told her audience in 1963, "Catholicism is opposed to the bourgeois mind" (*Collected Works* [*CW*] 862). O'Connor saw a deeper philosophical division between consumerism and Catholicism than between consumer society and the South. The Catholic novelist identified the "eternal and absolute" as her primary concern, her "true country" (*MM* 27). In these terms, in this "territory," resistance to consumerist values would be viable.

To affirm the possibility of dissent, however, O'Connor had to distinguish her form of religion from the ones that dominated American culture during the 1950s. *Wise Blood* attacks the dominant forms, suggesting that American religion had been appropriated by the "salesman's world." In the world of the novel, faith itself becomes a commodity. Charging a dollar for each new membership in the Holy Church of Christ Without Christ, Hoover Shoats urges his listeners "to take advantage of this church" (*WB* 154). The idea of the "new jesus" strikes Hoover as a lucrative one. "All it would need is a little promotion," says the self-proclaimed "radio star" (*WB* 156, 157). When Hazel refuses to make Hoover his partner, Hoover threatens him: "You watch out, friend. I'm going to run you out of business. I can get my own new jesus and I can get Prophets for peanuts, you hear?" Hoover will distort religious doctrine to suit his audience, but he adheres to one of the central tenets of capitalist society. "What you need," he tells Hazel, "is a little competition" (*WB* 159).

The marriage of capitalism and Christianity prompted expressions of disdain by writers other than O'Connor. A contributor to the *Christian Century*, writing in 1963, rejected the "spurious wedding" signified by the phrase, the "American Way" (Watson 329). For the most part, though, the American way in matters of religion met with uncritical assent. Like material prosperity, widespread religious observance was cited as evidence of American cultural superiority during the Cold War. In a nation concerned about the threat of "godless" communism, the civic value of religion gained general acceptance. All three branches of the federal government did their part to support a nationwide religious revival in the 1950s. Congress, for instance, passed legislation changing the pledge of allegiance to include "under God," and placing "In God We Trust" on all currency (Oakley 321). A month before his presidential inauguration, Dwight D. Eisenhower declared that "our form of Government has no sense unless it is founded in a deeply felt religious faith . . ." ("President-Elect" 16).

39

The religious aspect of American political rhetoric struck O'Connor when she listened to a radio broadcast of the 1956 Democratic National Convention. In a letter to Frances Cheney, whose husband served as a public relations officer for Tennessee Governor Frank Clement, O'Connor parodied the invocation with which Clement ended his keynote address: "All my subconscious has come up with this past week is Prahhhshuss Lord, take my hand and lead me awnnnnn!" (*C* 41).

In *Wise Blood* O'Connor incorporates lines of dialogue alluding to the Cold War alliance between nationalism and theism. Hoover Shoats tells his listeners they can trust his new sect, the Holy Church of Christ Without Christ, because "it's nothing foreign connected with it" (*WB* 152). Mrs. Flood suspects that the original Church Without Christ is "something foreign," and she will not show Hazel Motes a room in her boarding house until he assures her otherwise (*WB* 106). Such dialogue is in keeping with the insular attitude of the rural protagonist, who would have been content to remain in Eastrod, "with his two eyes open, and his hands always handling the familiar thing," and "his feet on the known track" (*WB* 22). But the dialogue also conveys the suspicion with which Cold War Americans viewed "foreign" ideologies, whether political or religious. They prized the "thoroughly American" faith described by a student of religious sociology in 1955. Will Herberg, author of *Protestant – Catholic – Jew*, called the American way of life "the operative faith of the American people." Herberg argued that the American way constituted the national religion, "the framework in terms of which the crucial values of American existence are couched" (88, 278).

At the same time, Herberg noted, several groups were unwilling to profess this "common faith." The "hold outs" included Catholics who refused to let their traditional creeds "be dissolved into an over-all 'American religion,' " and Protestants who espoused the "religions of the disinherited," or "the many 'holiness,' pentecostal, and millenarian sects of the socially and culturally submerged segments of our society" (Herberg 90–1).

The two varieties of religious dissent came together in the creative process of O'Connor, the Catholic writer whose fictional characters show the influence of Protestant fundamentalism. As a

Catholic novelist, she sympathized with "those aspects of Southern life where the religious feeling is most intense and where its outward forms are farthest from the Catholic . . ." (*MM* 207). In her fiction "the human aspiration" shared by Catholicism and fundamentalism (*MM* 206) unites them against the American way of life. O'Connor believed in an existential "framework" other than that of the American way: Christian dogma as "an instrument for penetrating reality" (*MM* 178).

A scene from *Wise Blood* is emblematic of the cultural scene in which religious dissent took place – when it did take place – during the Cold War. In the third chapter, Asa and Sabbath Lily Hawks interrupt the sales pitch of a street vendor and confront the people gathered around the man. While Sabbath hands out religious tracts, Asa rattles a tin cup and offers his listeners a choice between repentance and charity. "Help a blind preacher," he says. "If you won't repent, give up a nickel" (*WB* 40). His listeners have come downtown "to see what was for sale" (*WB* 37), and this intrusion of religious rhetoric into a commercial setting makes them uncomfortable; the small crowd begins to disperse. The vendor, who is selling potato peelers, yells at Asa: "What you think you doing? Who you think you are, running people off from here? (*WB* 40). After looking at one of the tracts, the vendor calls Asa and Sabbath "damn Jesus fanatics." Then, for good measure, he charges them with political subversiveness: "These goddam Communist foreigners!" he screams (*WB* 41).

A 1949 draft of the chapter, published as "The Peeler" in *Partisan Review*, places even greater emphasis on the link between religious suasion and political subversion. The vendor here refers to Asa and Sabbath as "goddam Communist Jesus Foreigners" (*CS* 65). If the political reference comes as a surprise in a narrative that departs so radically from "the customary kind of realism" (*MM* 40), the reasoning behind the reference seems more arbitrary still. At the time, however, the link was not uncommon. Indeed, it reappeared in the 1952 *Newsweek* review of *Wise Blood*. Along with "a satire on the secularization of modern life," the *Newsweek* reviewer found "a subtle parody of Communist soapboxing in Haze's street sermons." Hazel Motes never mentions politics, but the negativism of his message prompted the reviewer, undeterred by "the deliberate unreality of her tale," to read O'Connor's narrative as political commentary; the point about "Communist soapboxing" follows the observation that "the primitive evangelism" of Hazel's grandfather has become "purely destructive" ("Frustrated Preacher" 115).

For many of O'Connor's contemporaries, religious rhetoric that carried a message of "rejection" was politically suspect. Religious figures who failed to exalt capitalist society – pitting themselves against the cultural status quo and making a rival claim for the allegiance of American citizens – occupied a precarious position. In religious as well as political discussions, the totalizing dualism of Cold War rhetoric equated dissent with disloyalty. That is, with only two recognized alternatives, any form of dissent from the ideology of capitalism seemed to advance the opposite ideology, Communism. An essay by a Presbyterian minister, published in 1957, suggests that O'Connor's street vendor spoke for many Americans. John H. Marion observed that the "front-line participation" of American Christians in "certain sharp battles over social customs and group relationships" opened them to the charge of subversiveness when their convictions placed them "on the less popular side of these battles." Such "hard-pressed disciples," Marion wrote, "know that to buck certain powerful social forces . . . is to get oneself labeled, more than likely, as a 'fool,' a 'crackpot,' an 'agitator,' and maybe as a 'pro-Communist' " (91).

Marion's vagueness regarding "certain" battles and "certain" forces underlines the seriousness of the problem facing those who dissented on religious grounds. The specific issues on which they challenged the political consensus seemed less important, to those who upheld this consensus, than the challenge itself. In *Wise Blood,* the content of the street sermons hardly matters to the secular audience that is distracted from its window shopping. Asa Hawks seeks contributions more than converts, and Hazel Motes preaches against religious faith; but the mere fact that they speak the language of fundamentalist religion, calling people away from the consumerism that signified the superiority of the American way of life, alienates them from their listeners.

The shoppers in the commercial setting of downtown Taulkinham are not completely averse to religious rhetoric. They simply prefer the preaching of Onnie Jay Holy, who offers no challenge, actual or perceived, to their values. Hoover Shoats, who abandons his assumed identity when he advises Hazel on marketing strategy, keeps his message "sweet" to attract listeners and, ultimately, to collect money (*WB* 157). His sermons focus attention on the individual; his "up-to-date" church, he claims, calls forth "the natural sweetness" of the individual. What he counsels, then, is self-improvement based on positive qualities that have been suppressed by negative emotions. As a child grows up, Hoover says, "its sweetness don't show so much, cares and troubles come to perplext it, and all its sweetness is driven inside it. Then it gets miserable and lonesome and sick. . . ." When the individual learns "to unlock that little rose of sweetness," social success will result. Pointing to a baby in the crowd, Hoover cajoles his listeners: "Why, I know you people aren't going to let that little thing grow up and have all his sweetness pushed inside him when it could be on the outside to win friends and make him loved" (*WB* 150–1, 153).

O'Connor's own audience would have been familiar with this brand of religious rhetoric. Hoover sounds remarkably like the advertisers who promised individual distinction via material consumption, but his preaching also condenses a distinct body of spiritual counsel in postwar society. Hoover Shoats surpasses Hazel Motes in audience appeal because he speaks in the highly popular idiom of the "cult of reassurance," the movement to which O'Connor alluded when she criticized those Christians who "think faith is a big electric blanket" (*HB* 354). Norman Vincent Peale, the best-known representative of this postwar trend in religion, offered Americans a message almost identical to the one delivered by Hoover.[6] In his best-seller, *The Power of Positive Thinking* (1952), Peale preached a gospel of self-realization. "It is a pity that people should let themselves be defeated by the problems, cares, and difficulties of human existence," Peale wrote, "and it is also quite unnecessary." The solution, he maintained, was to stop thinking negatively about "your personal powers." Urging his reader to "believe in yourself and release your inner powers," he promised that "faith in your abilities" would bring success and happiness (Peale vii, 1, 16).

In effect the cult of reassurance translated the message of the 1955 *Life* editorial from cultural into personal terms: the individual was basically good, as American society was fundamentally sound, so there was no need for criticism. "This cult," Paul Hutchinson told readers of *Life* earlier in 1955, "says that the bedeviled victim of today's pressures should discipline his thoughts to reject all pessimistic ('negative') ideas and encourage optimistic ones . . ." (143). Such discipline narrowed the focus of religion to the merely personal, shifting attention away from society. For this reason a contributor to the journal edited by Hutchinson, the *Christian Century,* objected to the emphasis on "personal adjustment." A. Roy Eckardt wondered "how much the social order is *worth* adjusting to" and derided the cult for its failure to ask the same question:

> An evil aspect of peace-of-mind religion is its acceptance, by default, of the social status quo. An unannounced assumption is that the present condition of the social order is irrelevant to one's true needs and outside the scope of one's obligations. (Eckardt 1395)

John C. Bennett and Will Herberg suggested that the nationwide religious revival of the 1950s had produced an American "culture religion," which Bennett blamed for the "loss of any basis of criticism on our culture as a whole" (qtd. in Eckardt 1395). Herberg lamented the transformation of Judeo-Christian faith into "the cult of culture and society, in which the 'right' social order and the received cultural values are divinized by being identified with the divine purpose." Christian faith, he wrote, "can be used to sustain the civic religion of 'laissez-faire capitalism.' " In general, "the new religiosity pervading America" validated "the social patterns and cultural values associated with the American Way of Life" (Herberg 279–80).

O'Connor reaffirmed the value of Christian faith as a challenge to the status quo. At the same time, she acknowledged the obstacles facing those who would resist consumerist values. The desire for "the good things of life" worked against religious resistance, just as it worked against regional resistance; Catholics in America were no more immune to the desire than Southerners. "Where

Catholics do abound," O'Connor observed in 1963, "they usually blend almost imperceptibly into the general materialistic background" (*MM* 201). This observation kept O'Connor from exaggerating the cultural impact that religious resistance would have. She never argued, for instance, that the American Catholic could eradicate materialism and reshape American culture "in his image" (*MM* 200).

Nevertheless, O'Connor looked to the Church to provide the counterforce to American consumerism. In doing so, she exemplified a phenomenon noted by the historian Jackson Lears. Applying the concept of "cultural hegemony" to postwar consumer society, Lears has suggested that religious bodies, among other "mediating institutions," helped the individual to escape "absorption by the all-encompassing system" (48).[7] Allegiance to the Church opened the possibility of "inner resistance" to the agencies of public manipulation – the possibility that McLuhan, himself a Catholic, mentioned in *The Mechanical Bride* (144). Rejecting the stereotype of the Church as an institution with its own methods of manipulation, its own "brain-washed" public (*MM* 144), O'Connor allied Catholicism with individualism. The kind of individualism she endorsed, in her nonfiction, differed radically from the brand of self-satisfaction promoted by the cult of reassurance: "to know oneself is, above all, to know what one lacks," she wrote in 1957. "It is to measure oneself against Truth, and not the other way around" (*MM* 35).

In *Wise Blood*, admittedly, the True Faith seems as remote as true selfhood. Only one Catholic appears in the novel, "a Lapsed Catholic" whose belief in "eternal punishment" does not prevent him from visiting a whorehouse (*WB* 147). The few scattered references to Catholicism are disparaging. In a flashback Hazel declares his own autonomy: "no priest taking orders from no pope was going to tamper with his soul" (*WB* 24). When his landlady wants to insult Hazel, she accuses him of being an "agent of the pope" (*WB* 225). Clearly, the characters who inhabit the "salesman's world" of *Wise Blood* have little use for the Church.

Even so, its virtual absence from their world does not imply its irrelevance to the cultural conditions analyzed by O'Connor. Mrs. Flood insults Hazel because she suspects that he has abandoned his own "fine church," and their common materialism, for "something that he couldn't get without being blind to everything else" (*WB* 216, 225). Even from her limited perspective, the Catholic Church represents a system of values incompatible with the "salesman's world." The author who refused to evade ideological issues by escaping into a realm of aesthetic concerns – as many intellectuals had done – would hardly have accepted peaceful coexistence with consumer society. O'Connor keeps the Church at a distance from the world of the characters in order to preserve the integrity of the Catholic alternative. The Church corresponds to the "pin point of light" Mrs. Flood imagines when she tries to understand the change that Hazel has undergone, the change that has taken him "backwards to Bethlehem" (*WB* 218, 219). The Church illuminates the possibility of individual identity, which consumer culture both celebrates and destroys.

NOTES

1 Fredric Jameson has identified two theoretical positions on "the end of individualism" in consumer society: "The first one is content to say: yes, once upon a time, in the classic age of competitive capitalism, in the heyday of the nuclear family and the emergence of the bourgeoisie as the hegemonic social class, there was such a thing as individualism, as individual subjects. But today, in the age of corporate capitalism, of the so-called organization man, of bureaucracies in business as well as in the state, of demographic explosion – today, that older bourgeois individual subject no longer exists.

   Then there is a second position, the more radical of the two, what one might call the poststructuralist position. It adds: not only is the bourgeois individual subject a thing of the past, it is also a myth; it *never* really existed in the first place; there have never been autonomous subjects of that type. Rather, this construct is merely a philosophical and cultural mystification which sought to persuade people that they "had" individual subjects and possessed this unique personal identity" (Jameson 114, 115). O'Connor, like McLuhan, viewed "the end of individualism" from a perspective much closer to the first position.

2 For a discussion of this intellectual trend, see Lears 38–48.

3 Critics of the novel have sometimes oversimplified the question of

motivation by arguing that the characters act instinctively. One of the first reviews included this assessment of Enoch and the other characters: "They live, like animals, according to some anonymous law of the blood" (Simons 298).

4 In his book, *A Wreck on the Road to Damascus,* Brian Abel Ragen develops this argument at length (107–95).

5 Television struck many other writers as a sign, or even an instrument, of national cultural homogenization. In 1957 one of O'Connor's admirers criticized "the enforced conformity of modern industrial life, which measures its days by factory whistles and its nights by television channel changes." Television antennae, like "almost identical ranch homes in almost identical housing projects," signified the loss of Southern regional identity for Louis D. Rubin (13, 14). According to Jack Kerouac, television reinforced "middle-class non-identity." In his 1958 novel *The Dharma Bums,* Kerouac vilified the suburban home life that featured "television sets in each living room with everybody looking at the same thing and thinking the same thing at the same time . . ." (39).

6 In a paper delivered at the 1990 MLA Convention, Ragen noted that Hoover Shoats "reassures" his audience. Also, in passing, Ragen likened Shoats to Peale ("Soteriology").

7 Lears adapts the concept of "cultural hegemony" from the writings of the Italian Marxist, Antonio Gramsci (50).

WORKS CITED

Allen, William Rodney. "The Cage of Matter: The World as Zoo in Flannery O'Connor's *Wise Blood.*" *American Literature* 58 (1986): 256–70.

Burns, Stuart L. "The Evolution of *Wise Blood.*" *Modern Fiction Studies* 16 (1970): 147–62.

Eckardt, A. Roy. "The New Look in American Piety." *Christian Century* 71 (1954): 1395–97.

"Frustrated Preacher." Review of *Wise Blood. Newsweek,* May 19, 1952; 114–15.

Herberg, Will. *Protestant – Catholic – Jew: An Essay in American Religious Sociology.* Garden City, N.Y.: Doubleday, 1955.

Hoy, Cyrus, and Walter Sullivan, eds. "An Interview with Flannery O'Connor and Robert Penn Warren." 1960. In Rosemary Magee, ed., *Conversations with Flannery O'Connor.* Jackson: University Press of Mississippi, 1987. 19–36.

Hutchinson, Paul. "Have We a 'New' Religion?" *Life*, April 11, 1955; 138ff.

Jameson, Fredric. "Postmodernism and Consumer Society." In Hal Foster, ed., *The Anti-Aesthetic*. Port Townsend, Wash.: 1983. 111–25.

Kerouac, Jack. *The Dharma Bums*. 1958. New York: Penguin, 1976.

Lears, Jackson. "A Matter of Taste: Corporate Cultural Hegemony in a Mass-Consumption Society." In Larry May, ed., *Recasting America: Culture and Politics in the Age of Cold War*. Chicago: University of Chicago Press, 1989. 38–57.

Magee, Rosemary M., ed. *Conversations with Flannery O'Connor*. Jackson: University Press of Mississippi, 1987.

Marion, John H. "The Christian and Community Conflicts." In Malcolm P. Calhoun, ed., *Christians Are Citizens: The Role of the Responsible Christian Citizen in an Era of Crisis*. Richmond, Va.: Knox, 1957. 74–100.

McLuhan, Herbert Marshall. *The Mechanical Bride: The Folklore of Industrial Man*. Boston: Beacon, 1967 (originally New York: Vanguard, 1951).

Mills, C. Wright. *White Collar: The American Middle Classes*. London: Oxford University Press, 1951.

O'Connor, Flannery. *Collected Works*. New York: Library of America, 1988.

The Complete Stories. New York: Farrar, 1971.

The Correspondence of Flannery O'Connor and the Brainard Cheneys. Ed. C. Ralph Stephens. Jackson: University Press of Mississippi, 1986.

The Habit of Being. Ed. Sally Fitzgerald. New York: Farrar, 1979.

Mystery and Manners. Ed. Sally Fitzgerald and Robert Fitzgerald. New York: Farrar, 1969.

The Violent Bear It Away. New York: Farrar, 1960.

Wise Blood. 2nd ed. New York: Farrar, 1962.

Oakley, J. Ronald. *God's Country: America in the Fifties*. New York: Dembner, 1986.

"Our Country and Our Culture." *Partisan Review* 19 (1952): 282–326, 420–50, 562–97.

Packard, Vance. *The Hidden Persuaders*. New York: McKay, 1957.

Peale, Norman Vincent. *The Power of Positive Thinking*. New York: Prentice-Hall, 1952.

"President-Elect Says Soviet Demoted Zhukov Because of Their Friendship." *New York Times*, December 23, 1952, late ed.: 1, 16.

Ragen, Brian Abel. " 'And What's Dead Stays That Way': The Soteriology of the Church Without Christ." MLA Convention, Chicago, December 28, 1990.

A Wreck on the Road to Damascus: Innocence, Guilt, and Conversion in Flannery O'Connor. Chicago: Loyola University Press, 1989.

Riesman, David. *The Lonely Crowd: A Study of the Changing American Character*. New Haven: Yale University Press, 1950.

Rubin, Louis D., Jr. "An Image of the South." In Louis D. Rubin, Jr., and James Jackson Kilpatrick, eds., *The Lasting South: Fourteen Southerners Look at Their Home*. Chicago: Henry Regnery, 1957. 1–15.

Simons, John W. "A Case of Possession." Review of *Wise Blood. Commonweal* 56 (1952): 297–8.

Twelve Southerners. *I'll Take My Stand: The South and the Agrarian Tradition*. New York: Harper, 1930.

Watson, Kenneth. "The Myth of the 'American Way.' " *Christian Century* 80 (1963): 328–30.

Wells, Joel. "Off the Cuff." 1962. In Rosemary M. Magee, ed., *Conversations with Flannery O'Connor*. Jackson: University of Mississippi, 1987. 85–90.

Whyte, William H., Jr. *The Organization Man*. New York: Simon, 1956.

3

Framed in the Gaze: Haze, *Wise Blood,* and Lacanian Reading

JAMES M. MELLARD

THOUGH critics have questioned its integrity, read within the framework of the post-Freudian psychoanalytic theory of Jacques Lacan, *Wise Blood* demonstrates that Flannery O'Connor's fictional instincts are virtually flawless. Apart from the traditionally theological, the Lacanian reading provides a foundation for Hazel Motes's characterization, explains some of the otherwise hard-to-explain details of the text, and reveals the perfectly symmetrical structure of the narrative. A Lacanian reading, moreover, explains Haze's pathology, tracks the expressions of that pathology in his preoccupations with others, and shows that many of the specific details of O'Connor's text are more than merely stylistic or idiosyncratic. While every work of art must offer its own justification, justifications change over time, and any new interpretive approach must in some way highlight or bring one out for a new epoch. A Lacanian approach to *Wise Blood* does precisely that, finally, by showing how the novel is at once both modern and postmodern, a product of its own time (just barely past) and a meaningful work to be valued in a later one.

In this Lacanian reading, I want to assess Hazel Motes at the expense of others such as Enoch Emery. As every reader of O'Connor's novel realizes, Haze Motes is not an ordinary or "normative" subject. He is troubled, mentally. Indeed, he seems quite psychotic to most of us in his behavior. After all, he has no ordinary sense of sociality, no ordinary understanding of sexuality, no ordinary grasp of the immorality of murder. He operates by a code of values and behavior entirely his own. But as with every subject of this sort, the real question is why. Why does he behave as he does? What drives him? What is the etiology of his pathology? Although O'Connor, as Ben Satterfield emphasizes (33), always attempted in her public and private utterances to attribute Haze's "identity" to his drive for Christian redemption, in the novel itself she provides a perfectly legitimate psychoanalytic etiology for Haze's case. She provides, as it were, a case history. She gives us a scene of original trauma, provides the context within which we may trace that trauma's effects, and even "resolves" it in specific, formally consistent ways by novel's end. What's more, she does all this in ways consistent with aspects of Lacanian theory. For virtually every important element in the novel pivots on concepts we find explained in Lacan's notion of the gaze. Indeed, Haze and the novel are framed in the gaze.

1

The scene of originary trauma in *Wise Blood* does not occur in the first scene or chapter. It occurs in chapter 3. That traumatic scene first takes Haze (aged ten) to a carnival tent where he, apparently for the first time, sees a naked woman; then it takes him to the site of his mother's washpot and backyard fire where he expects to be punished for his sin and absolved of his guilt. This two-part scene is very rich in O'Connor's typical Christian and psychoanalytic language. But rather than analyzing it in detail, I want to analyze the resonances of the scene throughout the novel. The most important are the *textual* reminders of the register Lacan calls the Symbolic. These reminders become actualized in various ways in O'Connor's construction of Haze Motes as a subject. Because of their affiliations with Haze's pathology and the language of O'Connor's text, the most important of these is what Lacan considers the function of the gaze. In its being Symbolic and hinging on what is not there, the gaze brings some of the same conceptual difficulties as Lacan's notion of the phallus, which is not literally there either. Lacan's explanations range from the simple to the complex. In *The Four Fundamental Concepts of Psycho-Analysis*, Lacan says that the gaze is "others as such" (*FFC* 84). But he argues that the gaze is not really either the eye or another person looking. It is, rather, the field constituted by these and within which the subject becomes an "object," becomes, that is, subject to the gaze as a thing watched. The gaze, then, is an example of the Symbolic in action, for, like Lacan's notion of the Symbolic, it can be constructed only as a three-sided relation. In *Seminar I,* Lacan says: "I see that the other sees me, and that any intervening third party sees me being seen." Moreover, says Lacan, "It is not only that I see the other. I see him seeing me, which implicates the third term, namely that he knows that I see him. The circle is closed. There are always three terms in the structure, even if these three terms are not explicitly present" (218).

In *Wise Blood* O'Connor exploits this psychoanalytic structure in that crucial, formative, primal scene we have mentioned, but not assessed at length. She exploits there the gaze and invokes the Symbolic. No doubt reiterating the way in which Haze has objectified the naked woman in the carnival tent, the gaze that makes Haze into an object occurs the moment he returns home to face his mother. To begin with, the gaze rests with his mother, and the recurrences of the verbals "looking" and "watching" indicate its importance here. "His mother was standing by the washpot in the yard, looking at him, when he got home," O'Connor writes. Further, O'Connor suggests that Haze feels himself an object beneath the gaze and tries to escape it. But O'Connor's language suggests the authority of Lacan's concept. Since the gaze is not literal, one cannot escape it *in* the literal. "She was standing there straight, looking at him. He moved behind a tree and got out of her view," O'Connor tells us, "but in a few minutes, he could feel her watching him through the tree" (62). Thus, as the instrument that punishes Haze, the gaze is something to which he must consign himself. Consequently, with the associations of trees and cross insistently placing Haze amid Christic allusions, O'Connor writes, "He stood flat against the tree, waiting" (63). To Lacan, the gaze invokes the *structure* of the Symbolic. That structure, as we have said, is triangular. It is shown as triangular (as opposed to the linear, dyadic, dialectical structure of the Imaginary) in the text long before Hazel Motes grapples with it during the formation of his own subjectivity. In the structure of the gaze, where the "ego" and the first, "little" other (the ordinary person before our eyes) occupy the first two positions, the Other occupies the third position. It is the absent presence, the Symbolic presence that signifies the presence of the Symbolic.

Avant la lettre, O'Connor shows she understands this structure quite clearly. In many of her stories and both of her novels, she represents this Other-of-the-Gaze in the figure of Christ as One-who-watches-the-subject. That is the image she uses, for example, in *The Violent Bear It Away* at the moment when Tarwater, locating himself watching himself from Christ's position, understands he must baptize Bishop and become a prophet: "His black pupils, glassy and still, reflected depth on depth his own stricken image of himself, trudging into the distance in the bleeding stinking mad shadow of Jesus" (*VBA* 91). That likewise is the image found early in *Wise Blood,* where O'Connor says Haze "saw Jesus move from tree to tree in the back of his mind, a wild ragged figure motioning him to turn around and come off into the dark where he was not sure of his footing" (22). The same image appears in the "Author's Note to the Second Edition" of *Wise Blood:* there, Christ is "the ragged figure who moves from tree to tree in the back of [Haze's] mind" (unnumbered page). This image is also the one in the novel by which O'Connor represents Haze himself, the figure hiding behind a tree in order to escape the gaze of the first other (the mother) who enables the big Other. Within O'Connor's Christian view, Haze must get to the place that Tarwater reaches, the one from which he sees himself being seen, in order to understand that he himself incarnates Christ (just as, theologically, Christ incarnates God). But within Lacan's view, all that Haze must do is introject the Other as a Symbolic function that lifts him out of the dyadic oscillations of the Imaginary by providing a third perspective by which the others are anchored – to use Lacan's frequent metaphor *points de capiton,* or anchoring points. That third perspective is precisely the gaze itself.

Besides being a presence-in-absence, the concept of the gaze is as complex as that of the phallus because, in Lacan, the two are closely associated in the difficult concept of castration. Lacan says that the gaze invokes castration in the subject because the gaze reminds him or her that something (always, at bottom, the phallus) is lacking, that the subject itself is lacking something. Lacan explains what he means by the gaze in terms of vision, space, and perspective in painting. The modern notion of the subject (which Lacan eschews) that's so often represented in a visual position of control, he suggests, comes from the invention of three-dimensional perspective in art (*FFC* 86). That visual position Lacan calls the "geometral point." It is the conceptual point that makes three-dimensional painting possible. As it implies a prepotent determiner of spatial alignments that represent power and control, so also does it signify a human subject of power and control. Such a concept of the subject, Lacan suggests, becomes *the* representation of the Cartesian subject of Western thought. But that powerful, controlling, "privileged" subject is not Lacan's subject. His is one defined by his own interpretation of the relations of vision, visual space, and painting. His subject is precisely *not* the geometral point, though that point permits him to explain what his subject really is. Rather, Lacan's subject is one suggested by the entire field of the gaze, for the field of the gaze invokes not control or completion, but impotence, alienation or, in the Freudian's word, castration.

Where visual space seems split between the visible and the invisible, and so would seem to throw the subject-as-castrated on the side of the invisible, Lacan says, instead, "It is not between the invisible and the visible that we have to pass" as subjects beneath the gaze. Rather, the subject finds itself in the gaze located at the point of disappearance marked by the horizon. "The gaze is presented to us only in the form of a strange contingency, symbolic of what we find on the horizon, as the thrust of our experience, namely, the lack that constitutes castration anxiety" (*FFC* 72–3). Lacan insists that the subject can be constituted as a subject only through castration, the term that names the subject's recognition of lack and that institutes the desire that marks the subject's split. "The eye and the gaze," says Lacan, mark "for us the split in which the drive is manifested at the level of the scopic field" (*FFC* 72–3). Indeed, says Lacan, the scopic (visual) field is the one closest to desire because this field always represents loss or lack or absence. "In our relation to things," writes Lacan, "in so far as this relation is constituted by the way of vision, and ordered in the figures of representation, something slips, passes, is transmitted, from stage to stage, and is always to some degree eluded in it." That something is itself, says Lacan, "what we call the gaze" (*FFC* 73). Just as the subject cannot have the phallus, so the subject cannot "have" the gaze either.

2

O'Connor frames the entire novel within the gaze. She balances it, first and last, between images of the eye that function as a lure or as a screen for the gaze. Early and late, the eyes in question are those of Haze Motes. Moreover, the desire O'Connor represents in "minor" characters vis-à-vis Hazel in the first and final chapters, Hazel himself will have to encounter in the chapters between. In chapter 1, the other who peers into his eyes as if to find the answer to her being (which, for Lacan, *is* her desire *as* a subject) is Mrs. Wally Bee Hitchcock. When this woman speaks to him, O'Connor tells us that he neither answered nor moved "his eyes from whatever he was looking at" (*Wise Blood* 10). While she is inquisitive about his personal life, she finds herself strangely attracted to his eyes and tries "almost to look into them." O'Connor tells us "his eyes were what held her attention longest. Their settings were so deep that they seemed, to her, almost like passages leading somewhere and she leaned halfway across the space that separated the two seats, trying to see into them" (10–11). But those eyes resist her intrusion. The "color of pecan shells and set in deep sockets" (10), they are not a depth into which to look so much as a screen on which something will appear. That which will appear to her, though not in the eyes or their sockets, is like that which Lacan describes in Holbein's painting "The Ambassadors." "Holbein," says Lacan, "makes visible for us . . . something that is simply the subject as annihilated – annihilated in the form that is, strictly speaking, the imaged embodiment . . . of castration . . . [because castration] centres the whole organization of the desires through the framework of the fundamental drives" (*FFC* 88–9). Holbein achieves this effect, says Lacan, by reflecting "our own nothingness," the nothingness of the viewer, through the use of "the figure of [a] death's head" (92). O'Connor does likewise for Mrs. Wally Bee Hitchcock by using Haze's face as a picture into which to look for her self. O'Connor shows Mrs. Hitchcock instead "The outline of a skull under [Haze's] skin" (10). Had she herself eyes properly to see, this woman would perceive that what she sees is that she is not whole, that she, like the ordinary subject, is split, divided from herself, separated from that which she really desires. Haze's eyes, like Holbein's painting, become a trap for this woman's gaze. "In any picture," says Lacan, "it is precisely in seeking the gaze in each of its points that you will see it disappear" (89). What O'Connor's elderly woman desires is precisely that which disappears before her – the gaze as that which Lacan calls the *"objet a,"* an "object" that represents one's being.

However obtuse we find Mrs. Wally Bee Hitchcock in her inability to comprehend the meaning of the gaze she does not even know she seeks, we find her match in Haze himself. He has to encounter his desire, too. If the woman fails to understand at all her nature as lacking, Haze seems from the start to know his lack exists. As the elderly woman searches him for what she does not know she lacks, so Haze searches elsewhere for what he himself lacks and feels as a lack. Like the woman's, his quest focuses on others. Instead of regarding the woman who tries to gain his attention, "What [Haze] was looking at was the porter" (11). This man represents to Motes much that he knows is quite literally missing from his life. Haze imagines that the porter, despite his denials, is from his home town, Eastrod, and so, by association, represents for Haze the things lost from that hometown. In Eastrod he had once had a family and a community, albeit small. Now, the town, with its people, is gone. Once "there must have been twenty-five people in Eastrod" (20), but now there is no one. Moreover, he has lost each parent and both his brothers, and he dreams at different times in the sleeper berth of the burials of a brother and both father and mother. In their suggesting the focus of Haze's desire (desire for the gaze that represents his lack, itself always the phallus), the dreams have powerful Lacanian resonances. The dream about his mother is perhaps the most potent, for it most directly represents the phallus in the mother as phallic mother. It does so by representing what Lacan calls the "anamorphotic" power of the phallus when associated with the mother as still possessing the phallus (see *FFC*). In that guise as phallic mother, she represents once more the youth's demand to be punished, his need to satisfy the desire of the other, a desire that, of course, can never really be satisfied.

These significations emerge in the anamorphosis of the mother in Haze's dream. Haze sees her, we must realize, as something from a horror film, as, on the one hand, the living dead come back to stare at him, and, on the other, as the insatiable vampire of erotic demand who, unsatisfied in life, will find satisfaction somehow in death. Connecting to the power of the gaze, both images underlie Haze's dream-vision. First, "She would come with that look on her face, unrested and looking," O'Connor writes; it was "the same look he had seen through the crack of her coffin. He had seen her face through the crack when they were shutting the top on her" (26–7). But, second, O'Connor tells us, "He had seen the shadow that came down over her face and pulled her mouth down as if she wasn't any more satisfied dead than alive, as if she were going to spring up and shove the lid back and fly out and satisfy herself" (27). Though the coffin is shut on her, "He saw her in his sleep, terrible, like a huge bat, dart from the closing, fly out of there, but it was falling dark on top of her, closing down all the time." The anamorphotic distortions Haze's mother undergoes in his dream all represent some aspect of phallic authority. The horror of anamorphotic deformation, says Slavoj Zizek,

> lies not in [the] death mask, but rather in what is concealed beneath it, in the palpitating skinned flesh[. E]veryone who catches sight of this amorphous life substance has entered the forbidden domain and must therefore be excluded from the community[.] Therein consists the ultimate paradox of the "living dead": [it is] as if death, the death-stench it spreads, is a mask sheltering a life more 'alive' than our ordinary life. The place of the "living dead" is not somewhere between the dead and the living: precisely as dead, they are in a way "more alive than life itself," having access to the life substance prior to its symbolic mortification. Lacanian psychoanalysis locates the cause of this deformity in the anamorphotic gaze, i.e., the gaze sustained by an incestuous enjoyment: the anamorphotic distortion of reality is the way the gaze is inscribed onto the object's surface. (114–16)

Translated, these comments suggest that Hazel Motes is still beset by the desire of the (m)other, that he still must find some way to escape her devouring gaze, and that he must find an Oedipal Other, an Other of the Law, an Other who will properly impose the law of lack (that is, castration), in order to cure those horror-ridden dreams.

If those dream-images seem right out of horror films, then they may remind one as well that the escape from them lies away from the screen and back toward light. It is light, the point of light (one, not a thousand), that represents the *objet a*, the piece of himself that will save Hazel Motes. And it is the point of light that first suggests the Oedipal Other who will properly reify Hazel's castration. That point of light, indeed, is invested in the porter, the one (to play on the French in the name) who will carry him to his destination: the gaze as Other, the point of light as Christ. At first, still caught up in the Oedipal horror, Haze identifies with the perspective of his dead mother and so watches, as if in her place, the coffin close and the light disappear. Then, however, as we do from even the worst nightmare, he awakens, opens his eyes, and, trying as she had (in her shape as vampire) to escape from the burial box, finds himself (perhaps also a little batlike) hanging "there, dizzy, with the dim light of the train slowly showing the rug below" and "the porter at the other end of the car, a white shape in the darkness, standing there watching him and not moving" (27). The porter becomes indeed the object and the source of the gaze in the Other, the Other to which the text, in Haze's shouting "Jesus," gives a name. This point of light as the gaze will return at the novel's end, but the name given it then may well be Haze's own. Before he reaches that destination, he has to undergo many other trials, but they are all of the same sort. They all have most importantly to do with the gaze in action.

3

While much goes on in the novel that might draw our attention, it is Asa Hawks who focuses the theme of the gaze in ways most important for a Lacanian analysis. The Lacanian Zizek says that "the exemplary case of the gaze *qua* object is a blind man's eyes,

New Essays on Wise Blood

i.e., eyes which *do not see*" (117). Hawks illustrates this principle, for he shows that the gaze is not the eyes or, as Lacan says, "is not located just at the level of the eyes. The eyes may very well not appear, [or] they may be masked" (*Seminar I* 220). Hawks attracts Haze's attention because his eyes are masked behind dark glasses and, so far as Haze understands, do not see at all. Hawks is a "fake blind man" (111) in O'Connor's text, but his blindness is real enough to Haze until he discovers otherwise. Haze believes the man's publicity, a yellowed newspaper clipping Hawks shows him telling how he got the scars on his face and, presumably, lost his vision. "The headline on the clipping said, EVANGELIST PROMISES TO BLIND SELF. The rest of it said that Asa Hawks, an evangelist of the Free Church of Christ, had promised to blind himself to justify his belief that Christ Jesus had redeemed him" (112). The story so enthralls Haze that he steals the clipping, little knowing, as O'Connor tells readers, that a follow-up story says, "EVANGELIST'S NERVE FAILS" (113). While Hawks indeed had streaked his face with lime and made the scars, he was unable to blind himself. But it is neither Hawks's blindness nor his eyes as such that lure Haze to him. He is lured by what they signify – the gaze itself. "Generally speaking," writes Lacan, "the relation between the gaze and what one wishes to see involves a lure. The subject is presented as other than he is, and what one shows him is not what he wishes to see. It is in this way that the eye may function as *objet a*, that is to say, at the level of lack" (*FFC* 104). That lure is Hawks's face, which Haze desires to look into, and those eyes that signify Haze's lack, what he does not have, but wants. So the face and eyes are simply the screen that separates the visible and the invisible, the world of objects in which Haze exists and the world of desire into which he wishes to plunge. "He wanted to see, if he could, *behind* the black glasses" (145), O'Connor tells us, for no doubt he feels that there he will find what he wants, lacks, desires – the gaze itself, the gaze as Other, but, still, the gaze as "real," a something in the world.

The paradox of Haze's situation is that he longs for the gaze because he expects it to remove him from the world of objects and the gazes of others. But it is the gaze itself that makes him an object. "From the moment this gaze exists," Lacan tells us, "I am

60

already something other, in that I feel myself becoming an object
for the gaze of others" (*Seminar I* 215). That Haze feels himself
such an object under the gaze of others is shown in his dreams.
One (the "primal scene") we have assessed already. Another
dream occurs later and eventuates in Haze's waking encounter
with Hawks's face when the eyes are unmasked. In this second
dream-passage, O'Connor makes it plain that, despite Haze's con-
viction his salvation lies in the Essex he drives, the boxlike car is
as much a coffin as any other boxes the youth has encountered. It
is just another box in which to suffer the stares of others and from
which one must escape. Asleep in his car, Haze dreams of himself
as among the living dead, "not dead but only buried," and
awaiting "nothing" (160). Buried there, he sees "Various eyes
[looking] through the back oval window at his situation" (160).
Just as Freud says dreams often will, this one attributes the eyes
to the people with whom Haze had recently had contact, including Enoch Emery and the woman with the two little boys from
the zoo (in the dream, she offers him sexual favor). But the one
whom Haze desires to appear is Asa Hawks, for as signifier of the
Other in Haze's unconscious, Asa will have the power to free him.
But "the blind man didn't come" (161). So, awakening, Haze
decides to go to the blind man. He still longs to see what lies
behind Hawks's dark glasses. What he finds is – precisely – nothing. Well, he finds eyes that see, but in the context of the meaning
of the gaze they most certainly are not what he desires.

Hawks symbolizes the Other who, Haze believes, will anchor
his existence for him. Haze believes Hawks *has* what Haze desires,
the signifier of his redemption – the sign that he is redeemed, that
he can be redeemed, that someone believes in the redeemer Haze
tries to deny. That signifier is his very blindness, another screen
on which Haze projects the phallus he lacks and desires. But the
phallus, Lacan repeats constantly, can function only as veiled.
Unveiled, it neither functions nor exists. So when Haze sees
Hawks's eyes unveiled, unmasked, no longer covered by the black
glasses and returning his own gaze, that which Haze imputes to
the older man suddenly disappears. The scene in which all this
occurs exhibits the affective power of the primal scene, and as
such seems to repeat the primal scene represented in the carnival

61

episode. When he picks the lock to Hawks's room, the bodily reaction O'Connor describes is out of proportion to the physical danger. "He stood up, trembling, and opened the door. His breath came short and his heart was palpitating as if he had run all the way here from a great distance" (161). When he reaches the spot in the room where Hawks sleeps, "Haze squatted down by him and struck a match close to his face and he opened his eyes. The two sets of eyes looked at each other as long as the match lasted" (162). But Haze does not find there what he desires. "Haze's expression," O'Connor tells us, "seemed to open onto a deeper blankness and reflect something and then close again" (162). Except for a momentary glimpse of something reflected, perhaps a point of light, he finds emptiness, the emptiness of the gaze itself, "the strange contingency, symbolic of what we find on the horizon," "the thrust of our experience, namely the lack that constitutes castration anxiety" (*FFC* 72–73). In Haze panic ensues because, having invested his wholeness and autonomy in the blind man, he loses that investment.

Haze may give up on Hawks as the repository of the gaze that contains his being, but he does not immediately forgo the vision of himself as *something* constituted as a totality in the field of the gaze. While Hawks seems to represent a figure of the Other who will anchor reality for Haze, in fact Asa is just another figure of the father who, Haze learns, does not stand in the place of the phallic signifier, the signifier of signifiers. Thus Haze does not give up on apprehending himself in the gaze, that *objet a* which stands in for the subject as it stands in for the phallus, even though the gaze is the one thing the subject cannot grant. As Lacan says, "of all the objects in which the subject may recognize his dependence in the register of desire, the gaze is specified as unapprehensible" (*FFC* 83). What the subject aims to find in the gaze is itself in the point of light that makes the visual field possible. But the subject is not *there* in that point. That point is merely everything that looks at the subject (*FFC* 95) and in that look reifies the subject as an object that lacks and so desires, becoming indeed a subject because it desires, because it accepts its lack, because it accepts its not being there in the landscape of the gaze. In Lacan's analogy to "the picture," the subject learns "the picture, certainly, is in my eye. But I am not in the picture" (*FFC* 96). Haze has to understand that he is not in the picture, not in the field of the gaze, not in the landscape that comes under the view of the Other of the gaze. He learns that lesson, not in his disillusionment with Hawks, but in his loss of another object, the car that stands in for his mother, the mother-as-phallic-object.

The Oedipal Law forbids the subject to have the mother, and in that interdiction denies the phallus (which the phallic mother has). But Law, Lacan often remarks, is arbitrary. It can be Law only because it is arbitrary, something the subject accepts "just because," just because "the law is the law." This Lacanian theme "explains" one of the most troubling events in *Wise Blood*, one that virtually every critic has puzzled over. That event is the highway patrolman's wrecking Haze's car by pushing it down an embankment. When the patrolman kicks the Essex over the side, the action bears in upon Haze the implacable arbitrariness of Law and the immitigable loss of that which creates desire. The Essex gone, he is left with a picture, a scene, and, as Lacan would say, he is not in it. But death is. The scene he observes bears an emblem of death that, as it had when Mrs. Wally Bee Hitchcock saw it in Hazel's face, signifies his absolute meaninglessness. "The embankment dropped down about thirty feet, sheer washed-out red clay, into a partly burnt pasture where there was one scrub cow lying near a puddle. Over in the middle distance there was a one-room shack with a buzzard standing hunch-shouldered on the roof" (208–9). And after the car has been destroyed, the last thing he assumed to be a necessary organ of his existence has disappeared. So he is left with the "picture" itself, the landscape within which he might find the object that will give him meaning and identity. "Haze stood for a few minutes, looking over at the scene. His face seemed to reflect the entire distance across the clearing and beyond, the entire distance that extended from his eyes to the blank gray sky that went on, depth after depth, into space" (209). Finally, the nothing of space, apprehended through vision and the organs of sight, enters into Haze himself. Thereafter, he no longer has any *need* of his eyes and eyesight. Now we know why he blinds himself. In the sacrifice of his eyes, he gives up objects associated with what he has desired and thus, finally, yields his desire to the Other. Though he does not have to sacrifice his sight literally, the sacrifice has meaning nonetheless, for it says what kind of Other exists out there in the emptiness beyond Haze. "The sacrifice," Lacan says, "signifies that, in the object of our desires, we try to find evidence for the presence of the desire of the Other that I call here *the dark God*" (*FFC* 275). Given the nothingness of space and the nothingness of his own being, Haze transforms himself into the figure he had construed – or misconstrued – Asa Hawks to be. He *becomes* the screen on which others can project their gaze, the surface on which they may search for the object, the gaze, that represents them in their wholeness, the wholeness that always escapes one in life, but that in death, at least in the ideology of Christian afterlife, will not. Blinded and self-immolating, Haze becomes the Protestant saint O'Connor has belatedly foretold, foretold in the preface to the book ten years after its original publication.

4

We now return to the image of the point of light that, between chapters 1 and 14, frames the novel. At the end as at the beginning, we remain framed within the field of the gaze. That field defines Haze's redemption and the structure of the novel. Moreover, it eventually suggests why this modernist novel can speak to a postmodernist epoch. Read in modernist terms, the terms of the aesthetic ideology within which O'Connor wrote it, the novel offers "symptomal" meanings. That is, its surface "symptoms" hide "deeper" meanings our modernist reading can uncover. For the Freudian (who represents the model of modernist reading), the symptomal meanings are sexual. Sexuality is what's hidden. For O'Connor those symptomal meanings involve Hazel's desire for redemption. In a modernist reading (as readings, for example, by Asals and McCullagh suggest), the two are not incompatible. O'Connor has said in the letters that one of the most difficult technical feats her kind of fiction requires of her is the demonstration of "redemption" (*Habit Of Being* 118). In virtually every story, she has to find a way to suggest to readers that one character or another has achieved or failed to achieve redemption in her terms. Her solution, sometimes, is a fictional rendering of the Christian trope of "seeing the light." Because of the concept of the gaze, that image, like many others from the logic of O'Connor's Christian tropes, works perhaps equally well in Lacanian terms. In chapter 1, she invokes it negatively, but in the final chapter she uses it positively. In the two chapters, we thus find a similar structure of relations pivoting on the point of the gaze. As Mrs. Wally Bee Hitchcock peers at Haze while Haze looks elsewhere, to the porter embodying a point of light, so at the novel's end Mrs. Flood peers at Haze as again Haze, now in his blindness, looks elsewhere, to an image of the Other that we know, through his sacrifice, he has internalized. In his relation to Mrs. Flood, Haze in fact becomes the Other, both the object and source of the gaze. As the Other, he plays the role of the analyst in the dialogic relation to her. The analyst, Lacan says, in becoming the Other, becomes "the subject supposed to know," the subject one believes possesses the knowledge or the object one desires. We see this supposition in Mrs. Flood's feelings about Haze's blindness. Though she does not like to look at "the mess he had made" of his eyes, she finds herself drawn to gazing into the empty sockets, "staring into his face as if she expected to see something she hadn't seen before" (213). Suggesting that this woman is pure, prepotent desire, O'Connor's text tells us that because she could never look at anything long "without wanting it," she was "provoked" that the blind man saw "something" she did not have. "His face," O'Connor tells us, "had a peculiar pushing look, as if it were going forward after something it could just distinguish in the distance. Even when he was sitting motionless in a chair, his face had the look of straining toward something" (214). She takes this object toward which he strains as "a plan." "Why had he destroyed his eyes and saved himself," she wonders, "unless he had some plan, unless he saw something that he couldn't get without being blind to everything else?" (216).

But the modernist, symptomal reading uncovers more in the relation between this woman and Hazel Motes. In doing that, it begins to lead us to the more troubling postmodernist reading.

The modernist reading easily conflates the "hidden" messages of Freudian and Christian ideologies by showing that the desire of the Other, which will almost inevitably be cast in Oedipal terms, may also represent the desire for redemptive transcendence. The Freudian places that redemptive desire on the side of Thanatos. So do O'Connor's redemptive enfigurations. Her text suggests that in his role as Other, as the Lacanian subject supposed to know, Haze plays the role of the "dummy" in the card game of bridge. In Lacan's French, this dummy is called *"le mort,"* death or the dead (*Ecrits* 229). That is the role in which O'Connor puts Haze in relation to Mrs. Flood. O'Connor tells us that as she sits with him on the porch, "Anyone who saw her from the sidewalk would think she was being courted by a corpse" (217). In this role as Other, moreover, Haze ascends to the role of *the* Signifier, the symbol of omniscience, omnipresence. Merely a function of the role of the Other, this role is one that reifies, within O'Connor's ideology, Haze's function as Savior. In O'Connor's text this role is subsumed in the gaze, where subject and object, ego and other, may trade positions, where, too, the immensity of space may be subsumed in the tiniest pin point of light. Thus redemption lies in the subject's loss of ego-autonomy. As an unredeemed "subject," Mrs. Flood imagines that she is an ego in control, her head "a switch box [from] where she controlled" the other of reality (218). But as a "redeemed" subject, she finds herself thinking Haze's freedom is otherwise. "With him," O'Connor says,

> she could only imagine the outside in, the whole black world in his head and his head bigger than the world, his head big enough to include the sky and planets and whatever was or had been or would be. How would he know if time was going backwards or forwards or if he was going with it? She imagined it was like you were walking in a tunnel and all you could see was a pin point of light. She had to imagine the pin point of light; she couldn't think of it at all without that. She saw it as some kind of a star, like the star on Christmas cards. She saw him going backwards to Bethlehem and she had to laugh. (218–19)

Eventually, however, in Haze Mrs. Flood recognizes her own desire: she wants him or what he represents. Her story is clear. At first, she finds herself unable to think of anything else but Haze. For a time, as she becomes devoted to him and ministers to his needs more unselfishly than even she might imagine, she would stare at him at length, but she still saw "nothing at all" (222). Soon, though, her devotion becomes an office, a way of life – "Watching his face had become a habit with her," perhaps even a "habit of being." Finally, like Haze when he watched the face of Asa Hawks, "she wanted to penetrate the darkness behind it and see for herself what was there" (225).

"What was there" is the issue for both the modernist and the postmodernist reading. For the modernist as either Freudian or Christian reader, the hidden "what" is desire, the subject's desire of/for the Other, the father or the Father. Mrs. Flood, in the vicissitudes of her relation to Haze, represents both objects of desire. Imagining Haze as the master possessing some master plan, she herself had planned "to marry him and then have him committed to the state institution for the insane" (228). But that plan changes to include marrying and keeping him. Ultimately the plan dissolves and she loses herself in that selfless devotion to him. In her devotion she has cast Haze totally into the Symbolic. O'Connor shows that Symbolic role when his body is returned to Mrs. Flood by the policemen who have killed him. But she does not know he is dead, that he no longer merely plays the role of *le mort*. Dead, Haze is death, the Symbolic Other who, Lacan says, as Freud before him had said, always "knows." In that role, Haze leads this old woman to the place to which he had come when he had lost everything. In death, as a symbol of the Symbolic, he brings her to her own introjection of the knowledge of the Other. We uncover that knowledge in the two signifiers found in chapter 1 that neither Mrs. Wally Bee Hitchcock nor Hazel Motes had grasped – the death's head and the pin point of light. In these images we see that the "new jesus" Haze had sought and Enoch thought he had found in the mummy is now to be found in Haze himself. Observed by Mrs. Flood, his face shows the "outline of a skull," "plain under his skin" (231). Moreover, O'Connor tells us, "the deep burned eye sockets seemed to lead into the dark tunnel where he had disappeared." But as long as Mrs. Flood looks with her eyes she sees nothing. Closing her eyes, finally, and "looking" into that face she sees what Haze had seen. She sees that she herself is nothing in the gaze of the Other.

> She shut her eyes and saw the pin point of light but so far away that she could not hold it steady in her mind. She felt as if she were blocked at the entrance of something. She sat staring with her eyes shut, into his eyes, and felt as if she had finally got to the beginning of something she couldn't begin, and she saw him moving farther and farther away, farther and farther into the darkness until he was the pin point of light. (231–2)

Ultimately both the modernist and the postmodernist readings pivot on desire. In the modernist reading that has been the primary aim of this essay, both Mrs. Flood and Hazel Motes not only fulfill their desires, but those desires are acceptable to most readers. Both characters achieve "redemption." If redemption is a kind of truth, and truth for Lacan is "the truth of the subject," then Lacanian "redemption" is the subject's accepting its truth, its knowledge that one is split, lacking, alienated. Thus Mrs. Flood seems finally to reach that redemption. If so, moreover, she is the subject who demonstrates Haze's "redemption" through his transcendence of ordinary humanity. Because he is the agent of her ascendence *to* humanity, to knowledge that whatever we desire is always somewhere else, Hazel Motes ultimately functions as the Other, as, perhaps, the new jesus who can bring O'Connor's extraordinary grotesques to the truth of the ordinary subject. But in the postmodernist reading Lacanian theory also opens to us, some other, more horrifying, desire operates in O'Connor's text and in the relation of Haze and Mrs. Flood. This other desire is that not of the Oedipal Father, but of the "anal father," the grotesque figure, as Zizek writes of it (124–8), of the "little man" residing at the core of the subject and who represents, I suggest, the stumbling block of the (Freudian) sexual relation and the (Christian) redemptive one. Whereas the Other as Name of the Father permits the subject to sublimate Oedipal desire (the desire of or for the father), by making desire Symbolic, the anal father of postmodern reading makes desire real, places desire in the register of *the* Real where it resists the Symbolic, resists our repressions, resists our mediating discourses. This desire is that of the nightmare, the gothic tale, the horror film – and *Wise Blood*. This desire is not of the mother for the father, of the child for the mother or the father, but of the father for both – and more. *That* desire, the anal father's irrepressible, unsymbolizable, unmediated, totally *Real* sexual desire is what O'Connor's text, as *postmodernist* text, reveals to us in that grotesque, deformed, misshapen little man known as Hazel Motes. Though it might take an essay as long as this one to prove it, Haze is the terrible, anamorphotic, phallic thing that symbolizes O'Connor's horror not of sexuality (for that is constituted and controlled in our discourses), but of something more primal – of sex it*self.*

WORKS CITED

Asals, Frederick. "The Double in Flannery O'Connor's Stories." *Flannery O'Connor Bulletin* 9 (Autumn 1980): 49–86.

Lacan, Jacques. *Ecrits: A Selection.* New York: Norton, 1977.

The Four Fundamental Concepts of Psycho-Analysis. Ed. Jacques-Alain Miller; trans. Alan Sheridan. New York: Norton, 1978.

The Seminar of Jacques Lacan: Book I: Freud's Papers on Technique 1953–1954. Ed. Jacques-Alain Miller; trans. John Forrester. New York: Norton, 1988.

McCullagh, James C. "Symbolism and the Religious Aesthetic: Flannery's O'Connor's *Wise Blood.*" *Flannery O'Connor Bulletin* 2 (Autumn 1973): 43–58.

O'Connor, Flannery. *The Complete Stories.* New York: Farrar Straus Giroux, 1971.

The Habit of Being: The Letters of Flannery O'Connor. Selected and ed. by Sally Fitzgerald. New York: Farrar Straus Giroux, 1979.

The Violent Bear It Away. New York: Farrar Straus Giroux, 1960.

Wise Blood. 1952. 2nd ed. New York: Farrar Straus Giroux, 1962.

Satterfield, Ben. "*Wise Blood,* Artistic Anemia, and the Hemorrhaging of O'Connor Criticism." *Studies in American Fiction* 17.1 (Spring 1989): 33–50.

Zizek, Slavoj. *Enjoy Your Symptom! Jacques Lacan in Hollywood and out.* New York: Routledge, 1992.

"Jesus, Stab Me in the Heart!": *Wise Blood*, Wounding, and Sacramental Aesthetics

ROBERT H. BRINKMEYER, JR.

EVEN before its publication, *Wise Blood* was generating the type of heated controversy that continues to highlight commentary on the novel. When the editors at Rinehart, the publishing house that owned the option to the novel, decided not to publish it because of its unconventional and extreme nature (at least this is O'Connor's reading of the event), their decision looked forward both to the mixed reviews *Wise Blood* received upon publication and to the later critical wranglings over which critics still are fussing. Not surprisingly, early reviewers, most of whom knew nothing of O'Connor's religious background, focused almost exclusively on the bizarre qualities of the novel – the grotesque world, the repulsive characters, the wild goings on, the apparent meaninglessness of it all. The anonymous *Kirkus* review ended with a statement that spoke for a number of early readers: "A grotesque – for the more zealous avantgardists; for others, a deep anesthesia" (252). Later readers, aided by O'Connor's discussions in her essays and letters of the religious underpinnings and intent of her fiction, together with her author's note to *Wise Blood*'s second edition wherein she identifies Haze as a "Christian *malgré lui*" whose integrity lies in his not being able to escape from his haunting vision of Christ, have generally focused on O'Connor's daring attempt to communicate a Christian vision with repulsive characters acting wildly in a grotesque world. Whether Haze's actions are judged to be either completely meaningless or terrifically important pretty much depends on the critic's judgment of how successful O'Connor is in getting her Christian vision across. There is much disagreement on this score.

Much of this disagreement focuses on the apparent gap between the degraded world of *Wise Blood* and O'Connor's professed sacramentalism. In her letters and essays, O'Connor repeatedly wrote that her art and faith were uncompromisingly sacramental, celebrations of the world of matter because as God's handiwork it necessarily reflected the divine. O'Connor discussed her artistic sacramentalism in a letter (January 13, 1956) to "A.":

> I suppose when I say that the moral basis of Poetry is the accurate naming of the things of God, I mean about the same thing that Conrad meant when he said that his aim as an artist was to render the highest possible justice to the visible universe. For me the visible universe is a reflection of the invisible universe. Somewhere St. Augustine says that the things of the world poured forth from God in a double way: intellectually into the minds of the angels and physically into the world of things. (*Habit of Being [HB]* 128)

As John Desmond has pointed out, the foundation of O'Connor's incarnational vision is the Incarnation itself – the Word made flesh, the divine spirit assuming a physical presence in time and history.

Opposed to this incarnational, or sacramental, vision was the dualism of Manicheism that sundered spirit and matter. For O'Connor Manicheism was as much an artistic as a theological heresy. In "The Nature and Aim of Fiction," she stresses that only the "concrete details of life" make actual the ultimate mysteries, and so it is the artist's duty to work with these details and to resist the Manichean temptation so prevalent in modern thinking. In their dualistic beliefs, Manicheans find matter evil and degraded, devoid of spiritual significance, and so, as O'Connor points out, they seek "pure spirit and [try] to approach the infinite directly without any mediation of matter. This is also pretty much the modern spirit, and for the sensibility infected with it, fiction is hard if not impossible to write because fiction is so very much an incarnational art" (*Mystery and Manners [MM]* 68).

In "Catholic Novelists and Their Readers," O'Connor character-izes sacramental vision (what she typically calls prophetic vision) as a focusing of the artist's two sets of eyes, the artist's and the Church's. To see with only one set of eyes is to succumb to the Manichean temptation, sundering matter and spirit. O'Connor argues that for a Catholic writer to close his or her own eyes and attempt to see only with the eyes of the Church is to lose the world for the spirit; "the result," she declares, "is another addition to that large body of pious trash for which we have so long been famous" (*MM* 180). Equally destructive is the attempt to see only with one's eyes. "The writer may feel that in order to use his own eyes freely, he must disconnect them from the eyes of the Church and see as nearly as possible in the fashion of a camera," O'Connor writes. But "to try to disconnect faith from vision," she adds, "is to do violence to the whole personality," emptying the writer's imaginative vision of what O'Connor liked to call "the added dimension" of spiritual insight (*MM* 180–1). Only by attempting to see with both eyes, working to bring them into focus, does the Catholic writer see and write sacramentally. Achieving such a focus is for O'Connor never easy, since the temptation to close one set of eyes always beckons. "It would be foolish to say there is no conflict between these two sets of eyes," O'Connor writes. "There is a conflict, and it is a conflict which we escape at our peril, one which cannot be settled beforehand by theory or fiat or faith" (*MM* 180). The force that works to keep these two sets of eyes open, bringing their conflicting visions into focus, is O'Connor's sacramentalism.

Sacramentalism is likewise the cementing force of her faith. O'Connor repeatedly describes herself in her essays and letters as a believer always struggling with, rather than denying, her modern – and Manichean – sensibility. In a letter (July 20, 1955) to A., for instance, O'Connor discusses the dynamics of her Catholic faith, saying that she is "a Catholic peculiarly possessed of the modern consciousness, that thing Jung describes as unhistorical, solitary, and guilty. To possess this *within* the Church is to bear a burden, the necessary burden for the conscious Catholic. It's to feel the contemporary situation at the ultimate level" (*HB* 90). As she suggests here, O'Connor sees her modern consciousness, though troublesome, as "the necessary burden" for a deep and enriched faith; her doubt and unbelief, rooted in the Manichean dualism prevalent in modernist thinking, stand in resistance to simple adoration, thereby challenging, provoking, and deepening belief. To believe without acknowledging the questionings and torments of doubt is for O'Connor, as she wrote (July 16, 1957) to Cecil Dawkins, not to have faith at all but instead "false certainty." Such believers, O'Connor explained, "operate by the slide rule and the Church for them is not the body of Christ but the poor man's insurance system. It's never hard for them to believe because actually they never think about it. Faith has to take in all the other possibilities it can" (*HB* 231). For this reason O'Connor embraces her modernist consciousness and its tormenting challenges to her faith. Thus when, in a letter (May 30, 1962) to Alfred Corn, she identifies her foundation prayer of faith as Peter's appeal – "Lord I believe. Help my unbelief" (*HB* 476) – we should understand "help my unbelief" less as a call to assuage doubt than one to increase it so it can be overcome.

As with her sacramental aesthetics, O'Connor here locates the Manichean temptation at two opposing poles of her consciousness: skeptical modernism and unchallenged religious faith. The modern consciousness, O'Connor knew well, utterly devalues all existence outside itself in its radical subjectification of reality; with God dead, or at least entirely absent, consciousness becomes the god to be worshiped. J. Hillis Miller calls this drastic turn inward "nihilism," because it collapses the world into "the nothingness of consciousness when consciousness becomes the foundation of everything" (3). Such was a great temptation for anyone living in the modern world, O'Connor included, as her comment above to A. about her modern consciousness underscores. Unquestioned religious faith likewise empties the world of all significance since all values are located in the forms and structures of a belief that never confronts the goings on in here-and-now. Thus O'Connor's comment above that in never challenging one's faith a person "operate[s] by the slide rule" – religious belief becomes merely the working out of abstract formulas and equations.

O'Connor believed that Catholics were given to such resting easy in the security of their unquestioned faith. "Smugness is the Great Catholic Sin," she wrote (January 17, 1956) to A., adding, "I find it in myself and don't dislike it any less" (*HB* 131). To Sister Mariella Gable (May 4, 1963), she elaborated on this failing, saying that "our Catholic mentality is great on paraphrase, logic, formula, instant and correct answers. We judge before we experience and never trust our faith to be subjected to reality, because it is not strong enough" (*HB* 516). In part because they were in this regard strong where the Catholics were weak, O'Connor was an enthusiastic reader of the Protestant "crisis" theologians. In a letter (November 22, 1958) to A., O'Connor observed that there were now no Catholic theologians as powerful and creative as they, and as a result the crisis for Catholics was "losing the world" (*HB* 306) – an observation suggesting both a dwindling in the numbers of the faithful and the disappearance of the here-and-now in Catholic thinking.

Between these dualistic, world-destroying poles of modernist skepticism and religious smugness, toward both O'Connor admitted to being drawn, lay her belief in the Incarnation and the unity of matter and spirit that Jesus' presence embodied. Her sacramentalism was the force holding the opposing poles together, positioning them in healthy resistance that prohibited her from giving in to one or the other or from ignoring their temptations altogether. In the same letter to A. (July 20, 1955) in which she spoke of her modern sensibility as her necessary burden, O'Connor described her position as a Catholic in the modern world as a complex dynamic of suffering, doctrinal authority, and belief in Jesus:

> I think that the Church is the only thing that is going to make the terrible world we are coming to endurable; the only thing that makes the Church endurable is that it is somehow the body of Christ and that on this we are fed. It seems to be a fact that you have to suffer as much from the Church as for it but if you believe in the divinity of Christ, you have to cherish the world at the same time that you struggle to endure it. This may explain the lack of bitterness in the stories. (*HB* 90)

As forcefully as O'Connor condemns Manicheism and celebrates sacramentalism in her nonfiction, her fiction often seems to have more to do with Manichean dualism than sacramental unity, and this is particularly true with *Wise Blood*. Dogging critics of *Wise Blood* all along has been the problem of how to explain, in light of O'Connor's professed sacramental aesthetics and vision, the utterly degraded world of the novel, a world so fallen as to appear unredeemable. Except in the roadside signs proclaiming Jesus' power that Haze sees outside Taulkinham (and these after all are merely signs, signifiers of the absent signified), the only hints of the divine's presence appear in the distant heavens. One thinks in this regard of the frequently cited sentence describing the Taulkinham night sky which, as the narrator points out, everyone ignores: "The black sky was underpinned with long silver streaks that looked like scaffolding and depth on depth behind it were thousands of stars that all seemed to be moving very slowly as if they were about some vast construction work that involved the whole order of the universe and would take all time to complete" (*Wise Blood* [*WB*] 37). Or of the single cloud, "a large blinding white one with curls and a beard" that looms above Haze and Sabbath Lily during their drive in the country; as Haze drives home at the end of their escapades, this cloud, now "turned into a bird with long thin wings" (suggestive of the Holy Ghost), is "disappearing in the opposite direction" (*WB* 117, 127). Significantly, when Haze (apparently) ponders Jesus' presence and his commitment to Him after the patrolman has wrecked his car, he gazes not at the landscape before him but beyond into "the blank gray sky that went on, depth after depth, into space" (*WB* 209). There, and not in the world, is the realm of God – or at least so it appears.

With God absent, the world of *Wise Blood* is as grim and forbidding as its characters are grotesque and deformed. The boundaries that normally define and order existence are utterly askew. As Frederick Asals has shown, the narrator's use of metaphors that ascribe the animal and the mechanical to the human (Haze's face looks "like a gun no one knows is loaded"; Enoch looks "like a friendly hound dog with light mange" [*WB* 68, 44]) and of human qualities to animals and objects (bears in the zoo sit "facing each other like two matrons having tea, their faces polite and self-absorbed"; Haze's car "had a tendency to develop a tic by nightfall" [*B* 93, 154]), tears asunder boundaries between human, animal, and inanimate, yoking together disparate elements and categories. (37). William Rodney Allen, drawing upon Asals's insights, argues that the narrator's fusion of animal imagery with that of confinement intensifies what he sees as *Wise Blood*'s central theme – "that the world, without its spiritual dimension, is merely a prison for an odd collection of inmates – a zoo for the human animal" (257).

Making sense of all this mayhem in light of O'Connor's sacramentalism is a daunting task, as the efforts, or lack of effort, by these and other critics attest. Allen, for instance, painstakingly analyzes *Wise Blood*'s starkly despiritualized world but then generally ignores the knotty issue of locating O'Connor's sacramentalism anywhere in it. John Desmond, on the other hand, after brilliantly analyzing O'Connor's incarnational aesthetics, acknowledges that the reductive thrust of *Wise Blood* points to problems between O'Connor's imaginative vision and her narrative method; but then he all but dismisses these problems as merely the slipups of a young writer experimenting with comic satire. Thus, in looking at Haze's blinding and self-mortification, Desmond confidently claims that "the fact that his admission of sinfulness is not balanced by an explicit vision of the possibilities of redemption *in the world* does not negate the underlying meaning – the analogical action – of his progress and final stance in the novel" (57). Yet if a desacralized world offering no possibilities of redemption does not entirely negate the analogical action Desmond locates in O'Connor's incarnational art, it certainly deeply problematizes it, raising issues and questions that Desmond finally leaves unasked. In contrast to Desmond, Frederick Asals confronts these questions head-on, reaching the surprising conclusion that O'Connor's imaginative vision in *Wise Blood* was not sacramental but Manichean. "As we have seen," Asals writes, "the imagination that informs the novel does not perceive the 'physical, sensible world [as] good,' nor does it present clearly 'the image at its source, the image of ultimate reality,' that is the Christian God. . . . In short, rather than being pervaded by the 'Catholic sacramental view of life,' *Wise Blood* is in its deepest implications a 'Manichean' book" (58). Asals goes on to argue that O'Connor's Manicheism was limited to *Wise Blood;* in the fiction that follows, he asserts, O'Connor embraced, not without some struggle, a profound sacramentalism that dutifully accepted the world and corporeal life.

Asals's commentary is persuasive, but I'm nonetheless troubled by his setting *Wise Blood* off somewhere by itself, of his finding in it none of the sacramentalism that he sees (albeit in extreme manifestations) as O'Connor's signature in her other fiction. Although authors are not always their best critics, it is nonetheless significant that O'Connor never saw *Wise Blood* as being markedly different from the rest of her work — more extreme and angular in places, certainly; but created by a Manichean mind, certainly not. To Ben Griffith, O'Connor wrote (March 3, 1954) that *Wise Blood* was "entirely Redemption-centered in thought," and she assured him that "no one but a Catholic could have written *Wise Blood* even though it is a book about a kind of Protestant saint" (*HB* 70, 69). In a letter (September 20, 1952) to Betty Boyd Love, she declared without qualification, "The thought is all Catholic, perhaps overbearingly so" (*HB* 44). Asals and O'Connor give us two entirely different readings of the theological vision that structures *Wise Blood,* and the question I am pondering is whether we are limited to choosing between one or the other. Put another way: Is *Wise Blood* entirely Manichean or entirely Catholic, or can it somehow be both, Manichean and Redemption-centered?

I want to begin exploring this question by examining an issue that Asals raises in making his case for *Wise Blood*'s Manicheism (which he sees most obviously in "a repulsion at the physical deeper than anything required by the novel's motif of reverse evolution or the satire of a secularized society" [50]): the ascetic cast of O'Connor's imagination. Asals argues that O'Connor's deepest imaginative sympathies were rooted in the radical ascetic tradition that flourished before the Renaissance. Rather than attempting to reconcile what Asals calls the "major contraries" of Christian thought — "grace and sin, spirit and flesh, God and self, the heavenly city and the earthly" (200). O'Connor's ascetic imagination pushed them to their limits, forcing a stark choice between one extreme or the other. Asals points to the either/or choice underlying Matthew 16:24–5, a scripture central to the ascetic tradition: "If any man will come after me, let him deny himself, and take up his cross, and follow me. For whosoever will save his life shall lose it: and whosoever shall lose his life for my sake shall find it." There is no middle ground here.

For Asals, the asceticism of O'Connor's imagination typically stood in a healthy opposition to the sacramentalism of her faith; where the former pushed toward a sundering of contraries, the latter pulled them together, creating an ongoing relation of tension and resistance. The ascetic and the sacramental work against each other in a procreative dynamic not unlike the one Asals finds structuring sacramental thought, giving a depth and richness to O'Connor's fiction. "Out of the creative tension between the ascetic and the sacramental," Asals writes, "comes that mingled severity and radiance, the austere and the visionary, that marks the uniqueness of all O'Connor's later fiction" (205).

Asals argues that *Wise Blood* lacks the density and radiance of O'Connor's later fiction precisely because O'Connor did not pose her sacramental faith against her ascetic imagination and instead wrote entirely by the demands of the latter. Asceticism by this reading is a version of Manicheism, a literary and theological trap. Haze's violent self-mutilations for Asals thus represent "a thoroughgoing rejection not only of a secularized age but of life taken in through the senses at all – life in a world of matter" (56) and point to the Manichean conclusion that redemption is possible only in an escape from the physical, both the body and the world. Haze's asceticism as fanatic believer, for Asals, mirrors O'Connor's as extreme artist, with both giving into the Manichean temptation. In her later fiction, Asals argues, O'Connor continues to embrace ascetic dynamics (faith gained by purging and purifying the rebellious self) but for the purpose of achieving sacramental vision. The ascetic actions in these works lead O'Connor's protagonists back into the world rather than out of it, because what is purged and purified are not the body and the world but the consciousness that perceives them. With their cleansed perceptions of things, O'Connor's characters typically "are returned *to* a world of matter through which spirit gleams: the ascetic action thus comes to reveal the sacramental vision" (205).

By interpreting asceticism as a version of Manicheism that works against O'Connor's sacramentalism, Asals in the end shortchanges the complexity of *Wise Blood* and the richness of O'Connor's imagination. Rather than with Manicheism, ascetic dynamics share a great deal with those of sacramentalism. As Geoffrey Galt Harpham shows in *The Ascetic Imperative in Culture and Criticism*, the power of asceticism does not reside in the making of a stark either/or choice between Christian contraries, but instead, like that of sacramentalism, in the cultivation of these conflicting extremes in an ongoing interplay of dialogue and resistance. As Harpham persuasively argues, ascetic self-denial is not merely a simple act of purification of transgressive desires or aspects of the self, but instead the invoking of these transgressive forces so that through effort and discipline they can mastered. In this continuous pattern of calling forth and mastering transgression, the self gains insight and strength derived from critical self-awareness. Harpham describes ascetic dynamics:

> Asceticism both denigrates and dignifies the body, casting it at once as a transgressive force always on the side of "the world" and as the scene or stage for discipline, self-denial, ascesis. Only through certain physical acts acknowledged to constitute "mastery" over the body – as opposed to the body's mastery over the self – could virtue be acquired, attested to, or proven. . . . Ascetic discipline is a bodily act that points beyond itself, expressing an intention that forms, and yet transcends and negates the body; discipline makes the body intelligible by indicating the presence of a principle of stability and immobility within the constantly changing physical being. (xiv–xv)

In a similar line of thinking emphasizing the significance of the body in ascetic practice, Elaine Scarry argues that ascetic self-flagellation, rather than sundering the connection between body and spirit, actually enhances it, since self-mortification so insistently couples the metaphysical with the physical (34).

Harpham's and Scarry's readings of asceticism give us a way to understand asceticism not as a version of Manicheism but of sacramentalism – and a version that O'Connor, who always valued matters of the spirit over those of the world, found very appealing. While sacramentalism typically exalts the world of matter (particularly the external world) as infused with the sacred, asceticism generally exalts only the sacredly-infused body, not the world. Indeed, in its overwhelming emphasis on the body, ascetic self-denial excludes what Scarry calls "the middle term," or the world, self-mortification emptying the contents of the world of significance, in part because of pain's power to contract the boundaries of the universe entirely to that of the suffering body. By in effect canceling the world, asceticism thus highlights the direct relationship between the body and the sacred (Scarry

34). This world-destroying motion is not that of J. Hillis Miller's nihilism, because it is not the disembodied consciousness that reigns supreme, but the sentient body penetrated by the divine.

By this thickened understanding of asceticism, the dynamics of *Wise Blood* can be seen to be less Manichean than sacramental, though the novel's sacramentalism is one that cancels the world to celebrate the body. It is precisely this sacramentalism that Haze embodies in his mutilation at the end of the novel, one that stands in sharp contrast to the Manichean dualism he affirms up until his conversion. Before his final acts of self-mutilation, Haze, as a preacher of the Church Without Christ, strives to do everything possible to sunder forever the body and the spirit. His street preaching celebrates the pure body freed from any taint of the spiritual, as seen most clearly in his call for a "new jesus" who is "all man and ain't got any God in him" (*WB* 121). Haze's vision here of man who "ain't got any God in him" – a vision that Haze himself strives to emulate – points to the extreme strategy that such celebration calls for: the body must be totally cleansed of the spirit, which is not an ethereal, other-worldly force but a threatening physical presence within the body. As a teenager, for instance, Haze sees "Jesus move from tree to tree in the back of his mind, a wild ragged figure motioning him to turn around and come off into the dark where he was not sure of his footing, where he might be walking on the water and not know it and then suddenly know it and drown" (*WB* 22). Later, during his streetcorner preachings describing the illusory nature of the conscience, he nonetheless ascribes to it an honest-to-God body and asserts that for a person's own good "you had best get it out into the open and hunt it down and kill it, because it's no more than your face in the mirror is or your shadow behind you" (*WB* 166). Hunt down and kill is precisely what Haze does to Solace Layfield, Haze's mirror image, after he begins preaching under the hire of Hoover Shoats. Haze's murder of Layfield is anything but gratuitous, since he apparently sees Layfield as an embodiment of his own conscience, that part of him that knows Christ is true and that part that he has all along been struggling to extinguish in his preaching.

Haze's efforts to live entirely clean of the spirit are doomed to failure because the spiritual is so integrally bound up with the body that it can never be simply isolated and eradicated. Indeed, the very image of Haze's spiritual life – his "wise blood" – suggests that the mingling of the spiritual with the physical is what nourishes the body, makes it the living thing it is, alive both in the world and in the spirit. To live without the spirit is to become like the new jesus Enoch delivers to Haze – a dried-out and shriveled body of a shrunken man filled with trash. Because Haze's blood is always inescapably with him, his attempts to live a passionately lustful and happily depraved life are joyless and without any enthusiasm other than that of his singlemindedness to succeed. Sabbath Lily's taunt of Haze about their mutual filthiness rings true: "The only difference is I like being that way and he don't. Yes sir!" (*WB* 169).

As Sabbath Lily's words suggest, not everyone in *Wise Blood* suffers from the bodily presence of the spirit. Enoch Emery, for instance, like Haze, possesses "wise blood," but his is of an entirely different sort, not passed to him from God the Father but from his own father, and it pressures him not toward the divine but toward the bestial. Enoch's life is more instinctual than anything else; the narrator describes his thoughts – interior workings might be better – during a time when he knows his life has somehow been changed by the secret pulsing of his blood. "If he had been much given to thought, he might have thought that now was the time for him to justify his daddy's blood, but he didn't think in broad sweeps like that, he thought what he would do next. Sometimes he didn't think, he only wondered; then before long he would find himself doing this or that, like a bird finds itself building a nest when it hasn't actually been planning to" (*WB* 129). Lacking the searing presence of Christ that is physically a part of Haze, Enoch is utterly taken by Haze's call for a life entirely of the body, for that is the way his blood drives him. Haze stands in awe and envy of animals because unlike him they do not suffer a consciousness divided between intellect and instinct. Ultimately, when he dons an apesuit, Enoch descends to the bestial, giving in entirely to his wise blood. When Enoch buries his clothes before stepping into his bestial attire, the narrator comments that the act "was not a symbol to him of burying his former self; he only knew he wouldn't need them any more" (*WB* 196). Enoch, in other words, does not think in symbols and abstractions; like an animal, he acts entirely by instinct.

Critics typically interpret the motion behind Enoch's final acts as the inverse of Haze's self-mortification: Enoch moves toward pure bestiality, Haze toward pure spirit – the Manichean sundering. Haze's and Enoch's actions certainly contrast, but not in this way. Haze's abuse of his body, returning to Harpham's and Scarry's observations on asceticism, represents not a rejection of the body but a plunge into it, so that on a broad level his and Enoch's final acts are similar in their celebration of the physical. What is different is what they hope to achieve in terms of their spiritual lives by plunging into the physical. In his descent into bestiality, Enoch denies the spiritual to gain the world; he puts on the apesuit to overcome his alienation, hoping that people will reach out to him just as the crowds had to Gonga at his theater engagements. Haze, in contrast, seeks through his self-abuse to celebrate the union of body and the spirit, in the process utterly rejecting the claims of the world. Haze's violent self-mutilations collapse the external world into himself, paving the way for an unmediated relationship between the body and the divine. Even Mrs. Flood is aware of Haze's world-ridding motion. The narrator observes that she "could not make up her mind what would be inside his head and what out. . . . She could only imagine the outside in, the whole black world in his head and his head bigger than the world, his head big enough to include the sky and planets and whatever was or had been or would be" (*WB* 218).

Violent acts that cleanse the world of significance, paving the way for and announcing the entrance of the divine, occur throughout O'Connor's fiction, but typically these acts are not self-inflicted, even if the victims' self-pride is at times so obnoxious as to appear almost a deliberate invitation for some type of retribution. Any number of O'Connor's works conclude with bodily injury that signals the penetration of the divine: the goring of Mrs. May in "Greenleaf"; the grandmother's terrifying duel with The Misfit that brings insight – and death – in "A Good Man Is Hard to Find"; the striking of Ruby Turpin and her heavenly vision in "Revelation"; the rape of Tarwater and his acceptance of his prophetic calling in *The Violent Bear It Away*. While the significance of the world disappears in these violent acts, they nonetheless do not point toward a Manichean split between matter and spirit; rather, in shattering the characters' Cartesian worship of consciousness, they return the characters violently to their bodies into which the divine has somehow penetrated. Josephine Hendin argues that by burying the transcendent in the body O'Connor destroys the realm of the spirit; but actually the violent woundings in her fiction bring that realm into the body to enrich and transfigure – that is, if the characters accept this action of grace (29). Finally it is how these characters respond to their woundings in terms of reshaping their spiritual lives – and not how successful they are in terms of worldly success – that becomes the yardstick by which they are judged by O'Connor. It is this standard of judgment that O'Connor refers to in a letter (May 19, 1957) to Cecil Dawkins when she says that "the only concern, so far as I see it, is what Tillich calls the 'ultimate concern' " (*HB* 221).

The world-ridding, body-wounding (and celebrating) motion typical of O'Connor's fiction suggests that what Asals identifies as her ascetic imagination is both Manichean (world-destroying) and sacramental (celebrating the confluence of body and spirit) at the same time, marked by a charged interplay of resistance between the two perspectives. That O'Connor's imagination repeatedly moves to rid the claims of the world of any significance also points to the profoundly Hebraic cast of her vision that she in all likelihood acquired through her thorough grounding in the Bible and her profound sympathies with Southern fundamentalism. As Herbert Schneidau has so persuasively argued, the Yahwist vision of Hebraic culture (as expressed most vividly in the Old Testament) so devalues nature and culture before the looming, otherworldly presence of Yahweh that in a sense the world, the middleground between the individual and Yahweh, all but disappears. Schneidau cites the observation of archaeologist Henri Frankfort on the world-destroying power of the Yahwist vision: "Every finite reality shrivelled to nothingness before the absolute value which was God" (30). In a letter (October 20, 1955) to A., O'Connor spoke with approval of another correspondent's observation that, as O'Connor put it, "the best of my work sounded like the Old Testament would sound if it were being written today," noting that "the character's relation is directly with God rather than other people" (*HB* 111). The middle ground for O'Connor is finally worthless before matters of the individual and his or her spiritual life, a judgment that lies behind her striking observation that readers of "A Good Man Is Hard to Find" should pay no attention to the murder of the family but only to "the action of grace in the Grandmother's soul" (*MM* 113).

Yahwist, too, are the violent woundings of O'Connor's characters, woundings that she understood as actions of grace, penetrations of the divine into the world and specifically into the body. As Elaine Scarry has argued, religious faith in the Old Testament was substantiated in bodily transformations, typically either in procreation or wounding (in the New Testament, faith was substantiated in bodily healing and in the witnessing of the physical presence of Jesus). God in the Old Testament, observes Scarry, was generally conceived as a disembodied voice entirely separated from embodied humanity. Yahweh's weapons were the mediation between God and humanity; and it was through humanity's physical woundings by these weapons that Yahweh's presence became manifest (Scarry 198–210). Similarly, in O'Connor's fiction, wounding and bodily hurt announce and make known the divine. It's not merely, as O'Connor wrote (December 9, 1958) to Cecil Dawkins, that "grace changes us and the change is painful," but that before grace heals, as she said in a letter (October 10, 1960) to A., "it cuts with the sword Christ said he came to bring" (*HB* 307, 411). Such wounding is precisely what Mrs. Greenleaf calls for when, in "Greenleaf," she seeks Christ's healing powers by prostrating herself and shrieking out, "Oh Jesus, stab me in the heart! Jesus, stab me in the heart!" (*Complete Stories* [*CS*] 317).

In O'Connor's fiction Christ's sword manifests itself in any number of various weapons that injure and sometimes kill her characters; and generally it is only by being injured that Christ becomes real to them. "I have found that violence is strangely capable of returning my characters to reality and preparing them to accept their moments of grace," O'Connor wrote in some comments on her story "A Good Man Is Hard to Find." "Their heads are so hard that almost nothing else will work" (*MM* 112). The violence she speaks of here is not violence meted out by her characters to others but violence received by them; in O'Connor's world it is only with bodily injury that the self's true nature, freed from the everyday demands of the world by the body in pain, emerges to face the spirit and its demands. Thus The Misfit's comment about the Grandmother in "A Good Man Is Hard to Find": "She would of been a good woman . . . if it had been somebody there to shoot her every minute of her life." (*CS* 133).

Matters of faith as manifested in the injuring of others and of being injured are of course central to *Wise Blood*. As a boy, Haze strives to avoid Jesus because he fears the violence of his love. As we have already noted, Haze sees Jesus as a threatening figure "motioning him to turn around and come off into the dark where he was not sure of his footing, where he might be walking on the water and not know it and then suddenly know it and drown" (*WB* 22). Later, in his rebellion against Jesus, Haze strives to imitate his powerful injuring capability, delivering both verbal and physical abuse to just about everyone he meets. On the train ride at the novel's opening, for instance, he belligerently demands that the porter put away his everyday disguise and be who he really is, "a Parrum nigger from Eastrod" (*WB* 12) – a demand that mimics that of the all-powerful Yahweh for humanity's submission. The commandment Haze writes on his mother's chifforobe sounds like an edict from the Almighty: "THIS SHIFFER-ROBE BELONGS TO HAZEL MOTES. DO NOT STEAL IT OR YOU WILL BE HUNTED DOWN AND KILLED" (*WB* 26). Once in Taulkinham, Haze continues to threaten and to punish others. Even though in his preaching of the Church Without Christ he calls for a new jesus (suggestive of validating one's faith not by injuring but by witnessing), Haze lashes out with violence whenever he feels his religious message is threatened, as when he hits Enoch in the forehead with a rock, or when he slams the car door on Hoover Shoats's thumb, or when he runs down Solace Layfield with his car.

Haze's ultimate turning away from injuring others to injuring himself signals a tremendous turnaround in the thrust of *Wise*

Blood, a move metaphorically from the Old Testament to the New that signals a move away from Yahwist wounding to Christian healing. Jesus' presence no longer is manifested in an avenging weapon but in Haze's body, which through Haze's self-mutilations, becomes a copy of Christ's – a flesh-and-blood sign of the Incarnation in contrast to the disembodied roadsigns outside Taulkinham. It is the mystery of this transformation that Mrs. Flood somehow vaguely senses. As Haze through his ascetic acts seeks to master his body, seeks in other words to edit and purify the bodily text that proclaims Jesus through its copying of him, Mrs. Flood struggles to read and understand Haze's proclamation. The last chapter shows her faith slowly and fitfully emerging; her belief is not substantiated by her being physically injured but by her being witness to Haze and his mystery. She finds herself mysteriously drawn to her boarder, her down-home and selfish common sense, of which she is so proud, progressively giving way to something closer to kindness and charity. Before long, she finds herself spending most of her time sitting with Haze, watching and pondering – reading – the message of his emaciated body and wounded eyes. "Watching his face had become a habit with her," the narrator writes; "she wanted to penetrate the darkness behind it and see for herself what was there" (*WB* 225). At the end, with Haze lying dead before her, Mrs. Flood imagines him to be a pinpoint of light that marks the way for a journey she doesn't quite understand:

> She shut her eyes and saw the pin point of light but so far away that she could not hold it steady in her mind. She felt as if she were blocked at the entrance of something. She sat staring with her eyes shut, into his eyes, and felt as if she had finally got to the beginning of something she couldn't begin, and she saw him moving farther and farther away, farther and farther into the darkness until he was the pin point of light. (*WB* 231–2)

If Mrs. Flood, as the narrator's words suggest, is not yet ready to begin her own spiritual quest, she is also, as we can see in her development during the last chapter, much closer to that beginning. From the tempter of Haze, she has become something closer to his disciple, inspirited by his healing, not his wounding, power.

Haze's motion at the end – a plunge into the wounded body wherein matter and spirit are yoked together – typifies the motion underlying almost all of O'Connor's fiction. The radical displacements that characteristically close O'Connor's stories do not so much celebrate a world suffused by the divine as a body penetrated by it, usually manifested in a physical wounding. This action, as I have argued, is both Manichean and sacramental, with the world collapsed into the injured but now transfigured – or at least transfigurable – body. It's a central dynamic in O'Connor's Yahwist imagination that crucially shapes the thrust of her fiction from *Wise Blood* to her final stories.

In this regard *Wise Blood* is less an anomaly than a representative work. Ironically, what arguably sets *Wise Blood* off from O'Connor's other fiction is not the extreme nature of its grotesque and degraded world (as is frequently argued), but its final affirmation of faith not by being wounded by the sacred but by self-wounding (Haze) and witnessing (Mrs. Flood). Haze's self-mutilations, as we have seen, echo Christ's Incarnation, and Mrs. Flood's witnessing of Haze signals her spiritual evolution. This celebratory vision of Jesus' healing – not punishing – powers, carries the day here, an affirmation rarely achieved in O'Connor's stories, which are usually more recognizably Yahwist in thrust. *Wise Blood* is thus best understood as one of O'Connor's more extreme works; but its extremity lies in its openly incarnational conclusion, not in a Manichean rejection of matter. It therefore looks forward less to O'Connor's characteristically violent stories, such as "A Good Man Is Hard to Find," than to her occasional quieter ones, such as "The Artificial Nigger," where the transformations of Mr. Head and Nelson occur when they witness – and are transformed by their witnessing – a yard statue of a black man that in its suffering pose somehow radiates the divine. As punishing as *Wise Blood* is in places, its ascetic vision ultimately couples the body and the divine to celebrate the healing powers of the Redemption. While such a celebratory thrust lurks in almost all of O'Connor's fiction, it rarely is as visible and as forceful as in the conclusion of *Wise Blood*.

WORKS CITED

Allen, Willian Rodney. "The Cage of Matter: The World as Zoo in Flannery O'Connor's *Wise Blood," American Literature* 58 (1986).

Anonymous. Review of *Wise Blood. Kirkus* 19 (1952). 252.

Asals, Frederick. *Flannery O'Connor: The Imagination of Extremity.* Athens: University of Georgia Press, 1982.

Desmond, John. *Risen Sons: Flannery O'Connor's Vision of History.* Athens: University of Georgia Press, 1987, ch. 1.

Harpham, Geoffrey Galt. *The Ascetic Imperative in Culture and Criticism.* Chicago: University of Chicago Press, 1987.

Hendin, Josephine. *The World of Flannery O'Connor.* Bloomington: Indiana University Press, 1970.

Miller, J. Hillis. *Poets of Reality: Six Twentieth-Century Writers.* Cambridge: Harvard University Press, 1965.

O'Connor, Flannery. *The Complete Stories.* New York: Farrar, Straus and Giroux, 1971.

The Habit of Being: Letters. Ed. Sally Fitzgerald. New York: Farrar, 1979.

Mystery and Manners: Occasional Prose. Ed. Sally Fitzgerald and Robert Fitzgerald. New York: Farrar, 1969.

Wise Blood. New York: Farrar, 1962.

Scarry, Elaine. *The Body in Pain: The Making and Unmaking of the World.* New York: Oxford University Press, 1985.

Schneidau, Herbert. *Sacred Discontent: The Bible and Western Tradition.* Baton Rouge: Louisiana State University Press, 1976.

5

The Woman without Any Bones: Anti-Angel Aggression in *Wise Blood*

PATRICIA SMITH YAEGER

IN *Testimony* Shoshana Felman suggests that giving testimony or bearing witness has become "a crucial mode of our relation to events of our times," especially to traumas of contemporary history such as the Holocaust or the invention of the nuclear bomb. If testimony is one strategy for facing horror, it may also be an action that seems involuntary, that feels out of control. Even when we bear "witness to a trauma, to a crime or to an outrage; witness to a horror or an illness," the event itself may be so shocking that its "effects explode any capacity for explanation or rationalization" (Felman and Laub 1–6).

This is certainly the effect that Flannery O'Connor's fictions have on me. Reading her stories – for the first time or the tenth – I feel wounded, traumatized; I feel a simultaneous need to bear witness to the outward pain O'Connor's characters endure, as well as to the inward phantasm of my own body in pain. How can we rationalize Sabbath Lily Hawks's description of a baby's death in *Wise Blood,* for example? Do we excise it from our memory of the text, or do we sanitize it, torment it, until this anecdote seems to offer a clean, pure, uplifting vision of the morality to be attained when reading O'Connor's fiction?

> "Listen," she said in a louder voice, "this here man and woman killed this little baby. It was her own child but it was ugly and she never give it any love. This child had Jesus and this woman didn't have nothing but good looks and a man she was living in sin with. She sent the child away and it come back and she sent it away again and it come back to where her and this man was living in sin. They strangled it with a silk stocking and hung it up in the chimney. It didn't give her any peace after that, though. Everything she looked at was that child. Jesus made it beautiful to haunt her.

91

She couldn't lie with that man without she saw it, staring through the chimney at her, shining through the brick in the middle of the night."

"My Jesus," Haze muttered. (*WB* 52)

In this world without love, two grown-ups commit communal murder; they strangle a child who will not go away. But instead of injecting the reader with conventional horror, O'Connor suffuses this event with light; she makes the material world so transparent, so luminous, that the dead child begins to glow through the chimney, "shining through the brick in the middle of the night." What seems most unconscionable and horrifying about this passage is its aestheticization: its making of child-murder into something luminous or spiritual.

Reading O'Connor's fiction, we encounter these mind-numbing reversals on every page. A child murder makes us gag, not just because of the way that death is described, but because this death is made eerie or beautiful; or, an ordinary train ride becomes a form of assault as the train itself turns into a torture chamber:

> "Your feet in the middle of the aisle. Somebody going to want to get by you," the porter said, turning suddenly and brushing past.
>
> Haze got up and hung there a few seconds. He looked as if he were held by a rope caught in the middle of his back and attached to the train ceiling. (*WB* 12)
>
> . . .
>
> Haze laughed. The porter jerked the ladder off suddenly with a wrench of his arm that sent the boy clutching at the blanket into the berth. He lay on his stomach for a few minutes and didn't move. After a while he turned and found the light and looked around him. There was no window. He was closed up in the thing except for a little space over the curtain. (19)

O'Connor lacerates her characters; she pummels them to death, or turns on them with a grown-up version of the fury and power – the anti-angel aggression – she practiced against nuns and angels as a child:

> I went to the Sisters to school for the first 6 years or so . . . at their hands I developed something the Freudians have not named – anti-angel aggression, call it. From 8 to 12 years it was my habit to seclude myself in a locked room every so often and with a fierce (and evil) face, whirl around in a circle with my fists knotted,

socking the angel. This was the guardian angel with which the
Sisters assured us we were all equipped. He never left you. My
dislike of him was poisonous. I'm sure I even kicked at him and
landed on the floor. You couldn't hurt an angel but I would have
been happy to know I had dirtied his feathers – I conceived of him
in feathers. (*Habit of Being* [*HB*] 131–2)

Is this the sort of writing – or behavior – that we expect from one
of our finest modern American women writers?

In *A Room of One's Own,* Virginia Woolf suggests that twentieth-
century women's writing should bring something new into the
world; that remarkable things could happen to the English language if women described what really happens when they walk
into a room:

> One goes into the room – but the resources of the English language
> would be much put to the stretch, and whole flights of words
> would need to wing their way illegitimately into existence before a
> woman could say what happens when she goes into a room. (87)

For Woolf the absence of women's speech is extraordinary; she
imagines that a world of different objects and experiences would
come into view if only women could take up their pens and write.

> For women have sat indoors all these millions of years, so that by
> this time the very walls are permeated by their creative force, which
> has, indeed, so overcharged the capacity of bricks and mortar that
> it must needs harness itself to pens and brushes and business and
> politics. But this creative power differs greatly from the creative
> power of men. And one must conclude that it would be a thousand
> pities if it were hindered or wasted. (*HB* 87)

But what happens when Flannery O'Connor – or one of her
characters – walks into a room? The room itself seems to come
alive, to respond with the anti-angel aggression O'Connor invented in her childhood:

> The house was as dark as the night and open to it and though he
> saw that the fence around it had partly fallen and that weeds were
> growing through the porch floor, he didn't realize all at once that it
> was only a shell, that there was nothing here but the skeleton of a
> house. He twisted an envelope and struck a match to it and went
> through all the empty rooms, upstairs and down. When the enve-
> lope burnt out, he lit another one and went through them all again.

> That night he slept on the floor in the kitchen, and a board fell on his head out of the roof and cut his face. (*WB* 25–6)

Woolf imagines the walls of women's rooms permeated by creative force, but in O'Connor's stories this creativity lashes out at her fictional characters, punishing them, cutting into their bodies and minds. If Virginia Woolf was right about what women still have to say, we would expect a writer as stubborn and original as O'Connor to tell us something new about female experience, even when she is focusing on her male characters. But when O'Connor produces a story, what emerges seems treasonous and unexpected; it fits neither the stereotypes of Southern ladyhood that haunted O'Connor throughout her childhood nor the images of maternal jouissance or mutuality that have dominated recent feminist criticism.

To understand the sources of O'Connor's aggressive prose, I want to turn to another passage from *Room of One's Own* where Woolf contemplates a novel by the mysterious "Mr. A" – a man at the height of his scriptive powers:

> Indeed, it was delightful to read a man's writing again. It was so direct, so straightforward after the writing of women. It indicated such freedom of mind, such liberty of person, such confidence in himself. One had a sense of physical well-being in the presence of this well-nourished, well-educated, free mind, which had never been thwarted or opposed, but had had full liberty from birth to stretch itself in whatever way it liked. All this was admirable. But after reading a chapter or two a shadow seemed to lie across the page. It was a straight dark bar, a shadow shaped something like the letter "I." One began dodging this way and that to catch a glimpse of the landscape behind it. Whether that was indeed a tree or a woman walking I was not quite sure. Back one was always hailed to the letter "I." One began to be tired of "I." Not but what this "I" was a most respectable "I"; . . . but – here I turned a page or two, looking for something or other – the worst of it is that in the shadow of the letter "I" all is shapeless as mist. Is that a tree? No, it is a woman. But . . . she has not a bone in her body. (99–100)

It is this woman without any bones who will become the focus of my essay on O'Connor's *Wise Blood*. I will argue that O'Connor uses every strategy she can think of to avoid becoming or identifying with this female abject. At the same time, this destroyed, wounded, repressed, potentially dangerous female body – this body desiccated and pummeled by patriarchy, but also furious at its own disarray – haunts O'Connor's fiction. The forms it takes are unexpected. Although Woolf describes a writingscape similar to O'Connor's fictional landscapes, the surprise is that O'Connor identifies herself with, and borrows the strategies of, the well-nourished male writer. Like Woolf's poised, masculine narrator, O'Connor adopts a narrative voice that is confident, aesthetically pleasing, yet deeply sadistic (mimicking the censorious power of that "straight, dark bar" lying across the masculine page). Then she invents characters who serve as foils for this voice – who are always shadows of themselves, corporeal remnants, feminine or masculine others to pillory and punish – characters who must run from the sound of O'Connor's voice, but are always chastened by the force of her prose.

What does this textual schizophrenia tell us about O'Connor's status as a woman writer? O'Connor's letters reveal a curious refusal to allow herself to be gendered. In a missive written to her friend "A." in 1956, she explores the preadolescent sources of her writerly aggression:

> What you say about there being two [sexes] now brings it home to me. I've always believed there were two but generally acted as if there were only one. I guess meditation and contemplation and all the ways of prayer boil down to keeping it firmly in sight that there are two. I've never spent much time over the bride-bridegroom analogy. For me, perhaps because in the beginning, it's been more father and child. The things you have said about my being surprised to be over twelve, etc., have struck me as being quite comically accurate. When I was twelve I made up my mind absolutely that I would not get any older. I don't remember how I meant to stop it. There was something about "teen" attached to anything that was repulsive to me. I certainly didn't approve of what I saw of people that age. I was a very ancient twelve; my views at that age would have done credit to a Civil War veteran. I am much younger now than I was at twelve or anyway, less burdened. The weight of centuries lies on children, I'm sure of it. (*HB* 136–7)

This "weight of centuries" burdens the characters of *Wise Blood* on every page. Is this because its characters were invented by a deliberately childish persona – by an author trying to rediscover the pleasures and pangs of being pregendered: an author able to revel in an early, preadolescent anti-angel aggression that allowed unexpected acts of carnage and cruelty to emerge from the mind of an adult woman?

Instead of moving into her mother's role of imposing Southern matriarch, or agreeing to the abjection, the abysmal nonentity of the belle with no bones, O'Connor attempted, at least in her writing, to remain in the tomboyish role of the angel-aggressive little girl. While this choice may seem odd, I want to argue that it is a brilliant fictional strategy. In exploring this bizarre and admirable tactic, we will learn something extraordinary about what happens – and what has not often been acknowledged or described – when an angry Southern woman walks into a room. In O'Connor's case, rather than acting flirtatious or womanly, rather than upholding her community's norms by withholding her aggression, she begins to attack her society's angels; she picks up her pen and starts to write.

1. Surrealism and Childhood

Can we really describe O'Connor's lacerating prose as childish? Don't the verbal contusions she inflicts upon her readers (until the body becomes something less and other than itself – a wound, a corporeal remnant that cannot be integrated into the symbolic order of polite Southern society) seem all too sophisticated, all too grown-up?

In her essay on "Flannery O'Connor's Rage of Vision" Claire Kahane argues that a schizophrenic mix of grown-up sadism and infantile caprice is the hallmark of O'Connor's best prose, where narrator and protagonist become

> two aspects of one dynamic: the author's psyche, split into the punishing parent and the rebellious child. Thus most of [O'Connor's] protagonists, even when they are adults, seem fixed as children, – acting out a drama of infantile conflict in a context strangely isolated from social realities. . . . Paradoxically, it is because the narrator functions as punishing parent that she can dis-

tance herself from the protagonist and express the fantasies and forbidden impulses of the rebellious child. (58)

How does this rebellious infantilism, this strategy for releasing the child's brutal whimsy, work itself out in *Wise Blood?*

The story begins in a world bizarre beyond measure:

> Hazel Motes sat at a forward angle on the green plush train seat, looking one minute at the window as if he might want to jump out of it, and the next down the aisle at the other end of the car. The train was racing through tree tops that fell away at intervals and showed the sun standing, very red, on the edge of the farthest woods. Nearer, the plowed fields curved and faded and the few hogs nosing in the furrows looked like large spotted stones. Mrs. Wally Bee Hitchcock, who was facing Motes in the section, said that she thought the early evening like this was the prettiest time of day and she asked him if he didn't think so too. She was a fat woman with pink collars and cuffs and pear-shaped legs that slanted off the train seat and didn't reach the floor. (*WB* 9)

Mrs. Wally Bee Hitchcock, squat and helpless as an overweight child, is an outlandish miniature. She may seem "fixed" in her childishness, but she is also an adept at grown-up clichés. If she summons up visions of common sense and complacency, the world around her heaves with apocalypse. The sun, red and liminal, threatens "on the edge of the farthest woods." Dangerously personified, it mobilizes a world of metaphors: as it beckons, the hogs become stones.

Why does O'Connor invent this landscape brimming with paradox? Her opening points toward the bravura of epic: the ominous sun suggests a world waiting for heroic action. But the text also pivots between antithetical landscapes: the bizarre, apocalyptic sunscape is matched by the mundane world of sickly pigs – a world oddly junctured by Mrs. Hitchcock's voice. Here *Wise Blood* imitates the strategies of shock, alienation, and montage so typical of twentieth-century surrealism.

In *Notes to Literature* Adorno suggests that surrealist constructions "suspend the customary logic and the rules of the game of empirical objects . . . and bring their contents, especially their human contents, closer to the form of the object" (87). *Wise Blood* replicates this suspension of logic. While the sun approaches personhood, Mrs. Hitchcock's body approaches collage; like Mrs. Potato-head, she is made out of vegetable odds and ends, mixed out of her culture's flotsam and jetsam. Surrealism's affinity with dreams and psychoanalysis, its methods of displacing familiar objects with unfamiliar doubles or uncanny avatars can be a powerful aesthetic technique – not only because the uncanny plays on the unconscious, but because surrealist writing reaches into childhood. As Adorno suggests, surrealism represents

> the attempt to uncover childhood experiences by means of explosions. What Surrealism adds to illustrations of the world of objects is the element of childhood we lost; when we were children, those illustrated papers, already obsolete even then, must have leaped out at us the way Surrealist images do now. The subjective aspect in this lies in the action of the montage, which attempts – perhaps in vain . . . to produce perceptions as they must have been then. The giant egg from which the monster of the Last Judgment can creep forth at any moment is so big because we were so small the first time we looked at an egg and shuddered. (88)

As if to acknowledge her alliance with these lost moments of childhood, in the second paragraph of *Wise Blood* O'Connor zeroes in on a child's point of view:

> He looked at her a second and, without answering, leaned forward and stared down the length of the car again. She turned to see what was back there but all she saw was a child peering around one of the sections and farther up at the end of the car, the porter opening the closet where the sheets were kept. (*WB* 9–10)

One of the things that comes out of the closet in O'Connor's fiction is a frightening relationship between adult and child. The terrors of this relation emerge again when, examining the mummified man in the "Muvseevum," Hazel and Enoch Emery encounter a woman leading her two little boys. "She snickered and put two fingers in front of her teeth. The little boys' faces were like pans set on either side to catch the grins that overflowed from her" (*WB* 99). This dangerous female body, pressing into the child's physical space and threatening to obliterate its fragile boundaries, appears again in the titillating encounter between Hazel Motes and Mrs. Watts. As Hazel peeps through a half-open window, this aged prostitute and good-time girl becomes huge:

her scarey bulk recalls the giant bodies of grown-ups so threatening to children:

> He went up to the front porch and put his eye to a convenient crack in the shade, and found himself looking at a large white knee. After some time he moved away from the crack and tried the front door. It was not locked and he went into a small dark hall. . . .
>
> Mrs. Watts was sitting alone in a white iron bed, cutting her toenails with a large pair of scissors. She was a big woman with very yellow hair and white skin that glistened with a greasy preparation. She had on a pink nightgown that would better have fit a smaller figure. . . .
>
> He picked up her foot, which was heavy but not cold, and moved it about an inch to one side, and kept his hand on it.
>
> Mrs. Watt's mouth split in a wide full grin that showed her teeth. They were small and pointed and speckled with green and there was a wide space between each one. (*WB* 32–34)

O'Connor reinvents Wonderland's oversized Alice as happy Fauve princess – all yellow and pink and nauseating green. Only this time O'Connor doesn't reiterate Wonderland's silly euphoria. Instead, her text is infiltrated, penetrated, with the frightening perspective of the child for whom everything is overwhelming or exaggerated, whose body is always in danger. Thus when Hazel thinks of his mother, he imagines her both in her coffin and on the attack: "as if she were going to spring up and shove the lid back and fly out and satisfy herself: but they shut it. She might have been going to fly out of there, she might have been going to spring. He saw her in his sleep, terrible, like a huge bat, dart from the closing, fly out of there, but it was falling dark on top of her, closing down all the time" (*WB* 27)

Adorno suggests that surrealist objects seem huge or disproportionate because they reinvent the giant objects of childhood, "because we were so small the first time we looked at an egg and shuddered" (88). If O'Connor recovers this moment again and again in her fiction, it is not only to portray the child's helplessness, but to resurrect, as well, the child's canniness and rage. That is, her text is not only mobilized by the exploding world of the child-as-victim, it is also mobilized by the explosions, the revenge fantasies, of the victimizing child.

2. The Dead Game

To dramatize O'Connor's peculiar brand of regression – her delicious, disturbing resurrections of childhood aggression and anger – I want to describe my most recent encounters with infant sadism, namely, my three-year-old's invention of a puzzling ritual called "the dead game."

Last year my daughter invented a new sport that she tempted each of her babysitters to play. She called it "the dead game" – in honor of the quail chicks who died at her preschool the day they erupted from their shells. The dead game consisted of a single activity: my daughter pretended to be a corpse. She would lie on the ground, her tongue hanging out of her mouth and her eyes shut tight. The babysitter's job was to serve as spectator; to witness the repetitive fact of this infant death. Then my daughter would giggle, get up, and suggest that spectator and spectacle change roles; usually, the babysitter would demur, and suggest another activity.

This sparring with death – this game of loss, repetition, and resurrection – replicates the rhythms of O'Connor's prose. Think of the verbal relish, the pleasure O'Connor seems to take in creating the dead bodies in *Wise Blood,* a pleasure that approaches sensuality in, say, the scene where Enoch Emery gives the dried-up mummy-Christ to Sabbath Lily Hawks: "Two days out of the glass case had not improved the new jesus' condition. One side of his face had been partly mashed in and on the other side, his eyelid had split and a pale dust was seeping out of it" (*WB* 184). This weeping monster may be a pallid version of O'Connor's usual corpses, but it also invokes O'Connor's recurring fascination with mutilation and corporeal trauma.

Ecstatic at this invitation to play a new version of "the dead game," Sabbath Lily takes her slack-eyed memento mori and cradles him next to her body: "there was something in him of everyone she had ever known, as if they had all been rolled into one person and killed and shrunk and dried" (*WB* 185). The mummy-baby's corpse is not only sensuous in death; its bizarre particularity comes from a universal appeal: its status as a dead everyman. Even more remarkable, this corpse, who has already died a thousand deaths, shows a Christlike willingness to die again. Sabbath shows her new "baby" to Hazel, who

> snatched the shriveled body and threw it against the wall. The head popped and the trash inside sprayed out in a little cloud of dust.
> "You've broken him!" Sabbath shouted, "and he was mine!"
> Haze snatched the skin off the floor. He opened the outside door . . . and flung out what he had in his hand."
> He moved up closer and hung out the door, staring into the gray blur around him. The rain fell on his hat with loud splatters as if it were falling on tin.
> "I knew when I first seen you you were mean and evil," a furious voice behind him said. . . . "I seen you were mean enough to slam a baby against a wall. I seen you wouldn't never have no fun or let anybody else because you didn't want nothing but Jesus." (*WB* 188)

The horror of this scene is interrupted and intensified by its child-ishness, its simulation of a childish battle to the death over the corpse of a doll – as if to confirm O'Connor's vision of the youthful source of her writing: "I think you probably collect most of your experience as a child – when you really had nothing else to do – and then transfer it to other situations when you write" (*HB* 204).

In *Negative Dialectics*, Adorno suggests that this transposition of childish obsessions into grown-up speech may be more complex than we think; that children's fascination with death serves an extraordinary function. Children's irrepressible knowledge about the body and its fatality brings them closer to the philosophical meaning of the unspeakable – to events like the Holocaust – than even the most ardent philosopher. Adorno argues that those of us who live in the second half of the twentieth-century are on the brink of a new kind of philosophy, that the brute fact of the Second World War must transform our ideas: "The somatic, un-meaningful stratum of life is the stage of suffering, of the suffering which in the camps . . . burned every soothing feature out of the mind, and out of culture, the mind's objectification." After this, "in philosophy we experience a shock: the deeper, the more vigorous its penetration, the greater our suspicion that philosophy removes us from things as they are. . . . Life feeds the horror of premonition: what must come to be known may resemble the down-to-earth more than it resembles the sublime" (364).

If children inhabit this desublimated, earthly world, it is because children still feel

> the fascination that issues from the flayer's zone, from carcasses, from the repulsively sweet odor of putrefaction, and from the opprobrious terms used for that zone. The unconscious power of that realm may be as great as that of infantile sexuality; the two intermingle in the anal fixation, but they are scarcely the same. An unconscious knowledge whispers to the child what is repressed by civilized education; this is what matters, says the whispering voice. And the wretched physical existence strikes a spark in the supreme interest that is scarcely less repressed; it kindles a "What is that?" and "Where is it going?" (366)

This primitive fascination with death and bodily privation is the bedrock of O'Connor's fiction. And yet, this fascination is all too frequently redeemed by O'Connor's critics; her grim uncertainties become the source of religious festivity; they are transformed into a code for the symbolic sublime. O'Connor, the theory goes, is too good a writer to be obsessed with mangled corpses alone; her deviant prose reflects a lofty intent. "I think of Haze Motes as a kind of saint," she says in a letter to Ben Griffith. "His overwhelming virtue is integrity" (*HB* 89).

Most of O'Connor's letters support this insistence on "higher laws." O'Connor responds to accusations that she is a "writer of the realistic school" with high-minded acerbity: "I presume the lady came to this conclusion from looking at the cover of the drugstore edition of *Wise Blood*. In a few weeks I am going to talk to some more ladies in Macon and I am going to clear up that detail. I am interested in making up a good case for distortion, as I am coming to believe it is the only way to make people see" (*HB* 79). In letters and essays filled with humor and self-deprecation, O'Connor still manages to describe her own motives in smashing her characters and bashing her smart-aleck readers as principled and virtuous:

> I suppose the reasons for the use of so much violence in modern fiction will differ with each writer who uses it, but in my own stories I have found that violence is strangely capable of returning my characters to reality and preparing them to accept their moment

of grace. Their heads are so hard that almost nothing else will do the work. (*Mystery and Manners* 112).

Violence promotes grace; bad manners provoke moral awakening. At least, this is the cant about O'Connor's fierce fictions. But can we read O'Connor's ghoulishness another way?

After Hazel leaves Sabbath Lily and her shredded baby, he attacks Solace Layfield, a would-be prophet and alter ego, ripping into his body as if it were silly putty:

> The prophet began to run in earnest. He tore off his shirt and unbuckled his belt and ran out of the trousers. He began grabbing for his feet as if he would take off his shoes too, but before he could get at them, the Essex knocked him flat and ran over him. Haze drove about twenty feet and stopped the car and then began to back it. He backed it over the body and then stopped and got out. The Essex stood half over the other prophet as if it were pleased to guard what it had finally brought down. The man didn't look so much like Haze, lying on the ground on his face without his hat or suit on. A lot of blood was coming out of him and forming a puddle around his head. He was motionless all but for one finger that moved up and down in front of his face. (*WB* 204)

What's most haunting about these scenes is Hazel's lack of compassion. "Haze poked his toe in his side and he wheezed for a second and then was quiet" (204). Layfield begins a heartrending confession and asks forgiveness, but Hazel only gives him "a hard slap on the back," wipes the blood off his car, and drives away.

O'Connor's nearly clinical obsession with violence recalls a bloody anecdote from Slavoj Zizek's *The Sublime Object of Ideology*, where Zizek examines a disturbing scene from the cinematic version of *Parsifal*. In this movie the hero's wound is treated surrealistically: his injury is – quite literally – detached from his body and carried about on a pillow. Distanced from the body, this wound becomes "a nauseous partial object out of which . . . trickles blood" (77). Parsifal walks around toting a piece of himself, a wound that bleeds abysmally – sending shudders of curiosity and alienation up and down the audience's collective spine.

How do we read this dreadful image? Zizek suggests that our first impulse is to convert horror into symptom or symbol; to bind up the wound or deny it by inventing an elaborate moral allegory:

"The first, most obvious solution is to conceive this wound as a symbolic one: the wound is externalized to show that it does not concern the body as such but the symbolic network into which the body is caught" (79). Within this system the wound becomes a nostalgic memento, a detachable piece of the body politic symbolizing something rotten in the status quo – and suggesting that Parsifal's country, like his body, has fallen into "moral-symbolic decay" (79). This hyperallegorical code duplicates one of the critical codes for interpreting O'Connor's fictions.[1] Her wounds cease to terrify because they're designed to remind us of the fallen world; her characters sin violently in order to snap the reader into spiritual self-knowledge and frightened contrition.

But there is another side to O'Connor's stories; one that comes closer to the anti-angel aggressions she acted out as a child. Writing about the final death scene in "Greenleaf" she insists that:

> my preoccupations are technical. My preoccupation is how I am going to get this bull's horns into this woman's ribs. Of course why his horns belong in her ribs is something more fundamental but I can't say I give it much thought. Perhaps you are able to see things in these stories that I can't see because if I did see I would be too frightened to write them. I have always insisted that there is a fine grain of stupidity required in the fiction writer. (*HB* 149)[2]

Just as Zizek attempts another, "more radical reading" of *Parsifal*, I want to suggest a more radical reading of O'Connor's obsessions than either the religious-symbolic or "technical" explanation might allow.

Zizek argues that when we interpret Parsifal's wound as "a materialization of a moral-symbolic decay," we miss the way in which this wound functions as a spot or stain, as a moment that is incongruous, crisis-ridden, outside "the symbolic network of reality." Insofar as this wound "sticks out from the (symbolic and symbolized) reality of the body, the wound is 'a little piece of real', a disgusting protuberance which cannot be integrated into the totality of 'our own body' " (78).

O'Connor's fiction is filled with these "disgusting" protuberances. Hazel's glare-blue suit sports a price-tag, "still stapled on the sleeve"; his face refuses human integration:

He had a nose like a shrike's bill and a long vertical crease on either side of his mouth; his hair looked as if it had been permanently flattened under the heavy hat, but his eyes were what held her attention longest. Their settings were so deep that they seemed, to her, almost like passages leading somewhere and she leaned half-way across the space that separated the two seats, trying to see into them. (*WB* 10–11)

The bodies surrounding Hazel are struck with similar maladies. The porter's body swells with odd-shaped protrusions, while Mrs. Hitchcock's body zooms out of control:

She looked at him with her eyes squinted nearly shut. The knobs framed her face like dark toadstools. She tried to get past him . . . but they were both moving the same way. . . . Her face became purplish except for little white marks over it that didn't heat up. (*WB* 18)

Why this extraordinary focus on wounds, on protuberances, on body parts which seem to have a life of their own, which "cannot be integrated into the totality of our own body"?[3]

All of O'Connor's characters seem poised on the border of their condition as human beings. Their outer skins are a thin, tender layer, offering no protection from the poisonous matter on the outside and no protection from the abjecting contents within. Things happen to these characters that only happen in horror stories or animated cartoons. Enoch Emery gets a present from his father, a box with a picture of peanut brittle on the outside and letters that warn of "A Nutty Surprise!" "When Enoch had opened it, a coiled piece of steel had sprung out at him and broken off the ends of his two front teeth. His life was full of so many happenings like that it would seem he should have been more sensitive to his times of danger" (*WB* 178). Like Wily Coyote or Sylvester the Cat, Enoch Emery is caught in an eternal repetition: his body is always cartoonlike and on the line, always ready for victimization.

On his way to introduce Hazel to the new Jesus, Enoch resembles an escapee from a Looney Tunes asylum. He runs out the door with his landlady's defective umbrella:

Then to get it up again he had to place the tip of it on the ground and ram it open with his foot. He ran out again, holding his hand up near the spokes to keep them open and this allowed the handle, which was carved to represent the head of a fox terrier, to jab him every few seconds in the stomach. (*WB* 177)

The traumatic cuts that O'Connor's characters endure find their objective correlative in twentieth-century animation. This most childish of forms conveys meanings deep and devastating; cartoons present a ribald index to the condition of the human body in an alien and mechanized world. To see how this applies to O'Connor's fiction, we will need to explore the connections between O'Connor's deployment of the dramatic protrusions, the traumatic cuts riddling her characters' bodies, and her thematics of carnival: her flat-bodied approximation of the pleasures and the horrors of the traumatized bodies who inhabit animated cartoons.

3. Cartoon Bodies

If O'Connor's fiction keeps the prohibited impulse from childhood alive in her infatuation with the corpse, the bloody heap, with carnage, with the "dead game," this fascination with death and comic mutilation implies neither exile from nor refusal of the adult world of meaning and metaphysics. Instead she invents a new and startling entrance to this world; she insists that the self, the social body, is a kind of cartoon body that is the naked source of repetition, the painful site of traumatic cuts that detach themselves from the social and threaten – again and again – to become frightening corporeal remnants.

How should we characterize O'Connor's preoccupation with the corporeal leftover – with this trace of the body in pain? Zizek argues that any "openness" to social existence – to life as it is lived – may also be a form of self-laceration, since civilization distorts its subjects by imposing upon them a series of psychic cuts or deformities:

'By its own nature,' the psychic apparatus is not adjusted to reality: it runs following the 'pleasure principle' which cares nothing for the limitations imposed by reality; thereupon, the conditions of self-preservation enforce upon the psychic apparatus a renunciation of the absolute predominance of the 'pleasure principle,' its transformation into the 'reality principle.' The point not to be missed here is that the reign of the 'reality principle' is not something that the psychic apparatus could arrive at following the immanent, spontaneous path of 'maturation,' but something imposed, extorted by means of a series of *traumatic cuts*. (*Enjoy Your Symptom* 47)

What startles me most about O'Connor's fiction is its bold deployment of these traumas. As she cracks open or carves up every character in sight, O'Connor does things to bodies that prim Southern ladies should never imagine, much less write down. Even the unimpressive woman selling tickets at the picture show is menacing, with "corporeal remnants" tucked about her body at random. She "wore glasses with rhinestones in the bows and she had white hair stacked in sausages around her head. She stuck her mouth to a hole in the glass and shouted" (*WB* 105–6). These mysterious details "stick out" from the quotidian and indicate that something is amiss, that this body, like the other bodies that Hazel and Enoch Emery meet, memorializes "some strange, traumatic element which cannot be integrated" into ordinary reality.

In describing these wounds and protrusions with gusto, O'Connor also invents a clan of characters with the resilience of cartoon caricatures. Even approaching death, they move through the landscape like wind-up toys, experiencing disappointment with primordial vigor, as if somehow exempt from real pain. At the beginning of *Wise Blood* Hazel escapes metaphorical hanging; he survives the poisonous speech of the train-ladies while his body, already riddled with shrapnel from World War II, endures their sharp-nailed attacks. This deceptive immortality is the hallmark of animated characters, who fall from grace just when they seem most invulnerable:

Consider Tom and Jerry, cat and mouse. Each is subjected to frightful misadventures: the cat is stabbed, dynamite goes off in his pocket, he is run over by a steamroller and his body is flattened into a ribbon, and so forth; but in the next scene he appears with his normal body and the game begins again – it is as though he possessed another indestructible body. (Zizek, *Sublime Object* 134–5)[4]

107

This indestructible body has a limit in O'Connor's fiction – a limit that emerges at the edge of theology:

> There was already a deep black wordless conviction in him that the way to avoid Jesus was to avoid sin. He knew by the time he was twelve years old that he was going to be a preacher. Later he saw Jesus move from tree to tree in the back of his mind, a wild ragged figure motioning him to turn around and come off into the dark where he was not sure of his footing, where he might be walking on the water and not know it and then suddenly know it and drown. (*WB* 22)

If Jesus plays Jerry or Road Runner to Hazel's Tom-cat or Wily Coyote, Hazel is, of course, the fall guy, the character walking on water or air who suddenly loses his immortality and plummets to earth, obsessed with his precious cargo of flesh. While children may identify most consciously with the miniature Road Runner – that trickster imp who soars beyond the reach of the coyote's grown-up sadism – the fall guy can also be a source of identification. He represents the idiot motions of a core self, the subject of pleasure, appetite, and aggression who endures cut after cut in order to keep a grip on reality. This is to reiterate Zizek's lesson that the "reality principle" is not something that human beings discover as they travel along a spontaneous, organic, healthful roadway to maturation, "but something imposed, extorted by means of a series of *traumatic cuts*."

Cartoons have become the perfect modern vehicle for exploring and parodying these traumas. Walter Benjamin has argued that cartoons offer a particularly up-to-date forum, an extreme public space for exploring contemporary versions of the "reality principle." In cartoons the body seems comic and malleable, but it is really on the verge of tears, at the edge of its existential condition:

> The figure of Mickey Mouse answers to the historical experience of mutilation and fragmentation in technological warfare and industrial production. In 1931 Benjamin notes that the Mickey Mouse film upsets "relations of property": it visualizes, "for the first time, that one's own arm, even one's own body can be stolen." This bodily fragmentation, actually quite rare in Mickey Mouse, is more typical of "radical animation" in general: think of figures such as Felix the Cat, Koko the Clown. . . . the playful fragmentation of bodies in the cartoons forms a constellation with Dadaist depictions

of the body as a dysfunctional automaton or a dismembered man-nequin." (Hansen 44)

O'Connor's fiction is peopled with these dysfunctional automa-tons: "There was a steward beckoning people. . . . He was a white man with greased black hair and a greased black look to his suit. He moved like a crow" (*WB* 15). In O'Connor's world these human bodies change shape so quickly that they seem animated beyond the characters' command. As Hazel goes to his seat on the dining car, "the steward jerked his hand," and, puppetlike, Hazel lurches up the aisle, wetting his hand in someone's coffee. "The Steward placed him with three youngish women dressed like parrots." This constant mutability of forms moves the human body toward dismemberment. As these parrot-women threaten Hazel, their hands rest "on the table, red-speared at the tips." They make ugly sounds in their noses, blow smoke in his face, while a boxcar chugs past, chopping "the empty space in two." As one of women speaks in "a poisonous Eastern voice," the waiter dispenses more poisons: "something spotted with eggs and livers to eat" (*WB* 16–17).

Zizek suggests that "the symbolic order is striving for a homeo-static balance, but there is in its kernel, at its very centre, some strange, traumatic element which cannot be symbolized, inte-grated into the symbolic order – the Thing" (*Sublime Object* 132). O'Connor's prose pushes us toward this kernel of pain in unex-pected ways. First, her flat, cartoonlike characters make any per-ception of depth feel excessive, out of reach, so that profundity or humanity become acts of excess that seem surreal or supranatural, that don't fit the picture. Hazel's use of his mother's reading glasses – his sudden access to "wholeness" – only adds trauma to his body: "his head was thrust forward as if he had to use his whole face to see with" (*WB* 187). This opening up of psychic chasms in an otherwise flat emotional landscape is even more distressing when we hear Hazel's cough: "it sounded like a little yell for help at the bottom of a canyon."

In O'Connor's cartoon world, where people act like automa-tons, enduring the bizarre dismemberment or fragmentation of animated characters without knowledge or complaint, even the landscape carries an extra charge of corporeal excess:

> The highway was ragged with filling stations and trailer camps and
> roadhouses. After a while there were stretches where – red gulleys
> dropped off on either side of the road and behind them there were
> patches of field buttoned together with 666 posts. The sky leaked
> over all of it and then it began to leak into the car. . . . He had the
> feeling that everything he saw was a broken-off piece of some giant
> blank thing that he had forgotten had happened to him. (*WB* 74)

The "I" and the "not-I" are so close together in O'Connor's texts
that she dispenses an anxious, erotic charge; her leaky sky and
precipitous red gulleys threaten to break the body's boundaries.
This tinge of animation – this suggestion of a repressed, leaky
environmental eroticism – may cause us to forget, at least mo-
mentarily, how cruel and aggressive O'Connor's acts of character-
and object-mutilation can be.

In this reading of O'Connor, I have begun to suggest that her
enactment of these traumatic cuts, these "broken-off" pieces "of
some giant blank thing" that adhere to the self at every moment,
is not only dependent on her contact with a childish persona
capable of battering an archangel – but also on her willingness to
explore these crises as a grown-up woman writer able to invent a
poetics that can hold these cuts open. With this in mind, we can
return to our opening question: What does it mean for a woman
writer to invent this angry style, to write with so much aggressiv-
ity that she keeps this traumatic kernel, this corporeal remnant (of
Southern culture, of Western civilization, of childhood terror)
alive in her fiction?

4. The Woman without Any Bones

In *Killers of the Dream* Lillian Smith says that Southern language is
incredibly alluring – as soft and sweet as flesh itself. Its drawling
tones and euphonia soften the crises of Southern life:

> Our parents [indulged] us in a startling fashion. Poor and rich
> parents did this. We were petted children, not puritans. Sugar-tit
> words and sugar-tit experiences too often made of our minds and
> manners a fatty tissue that hid the sharp rickety bones of our souls.
> *Honey, sugar, sweetie* were milk names that still cling to our middle-
> aged vocabulary. Kisses and big hugs, and soothing laps to nuzzle
> up in, and tea cakes and bread 'n' butter 'n' sugar, and cane syrup

poured on hot buttered biscuit, and homemade ice cream and praise, gave a velvety texture to childhood which did not keep out the sharp stabs from the lessons but soften them now in our memory until we deny that we felt them at all. . . . how can one dig down deep enough into such a childhood to find the sharp needling lessons that sometimes gave a death-prick to our souls! (93)

If Lillian Smith defines a Southern speech or Southern body without any bones, O'Connor's prose digs deeper still and discovers the "sharp needling lessons" that make these bones start to sing. In a letter to Catherine Carver, O'Connor refuses the niceties of "sugar-tit words":

I have just got through talking to one of our honorable regional (with a vengeance) bodies. . . . After my talk, one lady shook my hand and said, "That was such a nice dispensation you gave us, honey." Another said, "What's wrong with your leg, sugar?" I'll be real glad when I get too old for them to sugar me. (*HB* 119–20)

Unlike Woolf's woman without any bones, O'Connor refuses to be undone by the "straight, dark bar" of this southern "I." At the same time, the powerlessness – and the anger – of the woman without any bones remains very close to the surface of her prose:

He went through the flap of the tent and inside there was another tent and he went through that. All he could see were the backs of the men. He climbed up on a bench and looked over their heads. They were looking down into a lowered place where something white was lying, squirming a little, in a box lined with black cloth. For a second he thought it was a skinned animal and then he saw it was a woman. She was fat and she had a face like an ordinary woman except there was a mole on the corner of her lip, that moved when she grinned, and one on her side. (*WB* 62)

O'Connor's women inhabit the border between humans and animals; abjected beings, even when they seem very powerful, these women confront us "with those fragile states where man strays on the territories of [the] animal," and may suggest O'Connor's own attempt "to release the hold of maternal entity" (Kristeva 12–13).[5] Hazel's penalty for viewing this squirming body is a brutal lashing from his mother. She, in turn, is excoriated by O'Connor's prose – shut up in her coffin, she flies out like a bat to terrify her son; but she is also obstructed in the dark, the coffin lid "coming closer closer down and cutting off the light and the room" (*WB* 27).

In her letters O'Connor portrays herself – comically – as a good girl barely able to censor the bad girl who rages within. But this bad girl *does* emerge in her prose, not only in characters like Hulga and Mary Grace, who appear in the later stories – but in those bizarre bodily fragments, those "nauseous partial objects" I've begun to describe: that series of wounds and protrusions threatening O'Connor's characters on every page. O'Connor haunts her own fictions, then, as "a little piece of real," an uncanny, unassimilable protrusion "which cannot be integrated into the totality" of the body politic (78).[6] This is to argue that the angel-aggressive little girl comes to life as spot or stain on the surface of Southern culture, as a character (or a part of a character) who "sticks out," who does not "fit" into the symbolic network that surrounds her.

Is this why O'Connor returns repeatedly in *Wise Blood* to a vast, unassimilable female body that takes up lots of space, but is also incarcerated or restricted: immobilized in a coffin or room of her own? In saying this, I am not suggesting a lamentable regression on O'Connor's part, but a powerful strategy for bringing an illegitimate voice into speech – a female voice whose capacity for anger, aggression, and sheer ornery meanness had not been explored until O'Connor began to write. O'Connor's fictions suggest that something quite fascinating can happen when the female body is repressed or cut into: when the little girl is asked by her culture to give up her aggression or rebellion, she can, in fact, cut back.

Longing, even as a grown woman, to grow up, to be "too old for them to sugar me," O'Connor plots the demise of these repressive Southern matrons by writing a prose more brutal, more violent, than any of her contemporaries could have imagined:

> The outline of a skull was plain under his skin and the deep burned eye sockets seemed to lead into the dark tunnel where he had disappeared. She leaned closer and closer to his face, looking deep into them, trying to see how she had been cheated or what had cheated her, but she couldn't see anything. She shut her eyes and saw the pin point of light but so far away that she could not hold it steady in her mind. She felt as if she were blocked at the entrance of something. She sat staring with her eyes shut, into his eyes, and felt as if she had finally got to the beginning of something she

couldn't begin, and she saw him moving farther and farther away, farther and farther into the darkness until he was the pin point of light. (231–2)

In considering the religious sources of O'Connor's prose – her elegant and alien retelling of the Christ myth through Hazel Motes, as he offers up his body and suggests a violent path that might permit his landlady to be redeemed – we should not lose sight of the metaphorics of violence and blockage this passage also represents.[7] Like the woman without any bones, the landlady is "blocked at the entrance of something"; she has reached through to the "beginning of something she couldn't begin." At the site of her blockage we find the man with no bones; or better, the man with too many bones. But in this place where we encounter vestiges of the anxiety of authorship that feminist critics like Gilbert and Gubar have discovered as a tie binding women writers, we also encounter a male muse who ceases to block a feminine quester, but beckons her to come to the other side. This beckoning may be terrifying, it may be far from the flowery fields of the heterosexual romance that fuels patriarchal prosody. Instead O'Connor takes a wry pleasure in sticking it to her hero and heroine alike; she has chosen a particular remedy for cultural blockage by recovering an incredible fount of life-saving, script-saving anger. What gets called upon in O'Connor's prose is the aggression and feistiness of the preadolescent girl who refuses, especially in *Wise Blood,* to cleave to any serene standard of female decorum or beauty, but batters her society's angels without ceasing.

In exiling Hazel Motes, O'Connor responds to one version of her own guardian-angel anxiety. In spiritually crucifying his landlady, she batters another set of clichés and parodies another local angel. Finally, by stranding Enoch Emery in his monkey suit, she refuses to embrace the female plot of care and connection, of love and ritual, that has become a staple of women's fiction. O'Connor does not offer, then, the portrait of an idealized female writer; she is someone more interesting, an angel-aggressive woman who uses her violent imaginary and her wicked sense of humor to change the balance of social power and create a new form of writing as antiritual. This antiritual involves forms of violence and self-knowledge native to childhood:

That this has been forgotten, that we no longer know what we used to feel before the dogcatcher's van, is both the triumph of culture and its failure. Culture, which keeps emulating the old Adam, cannot bear to be reminded of that zone, and precisely this is not to be reconciled with the conception that culture has of itself. It abhors stench because it stinks – because, as Brecht put it in a magnificent line, its mansion is built of dogshit. Years after that line was written, Auschwitz demonstrated irrefutably that culture has failed. (366)

Adorno equates a fascination with death and self-consciousness about culture's wounds with the lost recognitions of the angry and terrified child. O'Connor makes a similar point about the terrors of modern culture in a letter to "A.":

I am reading Eichmann in Jerusalem, which Tom [Stritch] sent me. Anything is credible after such a period of history. I've always been haunted by the boxcars, but they were actually the least of it. (*HB* 539)

In O'Connor's first novel, cartoon characters and maimed spirits evoke these now-emptied boxcars; they also cavort around the woman writer's lost bones and reawaken her anger, as she sings about the terror and loss we must endure as we continue into the twenty-first century.

NOTES

1 For readings of O'Connor that open new territory, see especially Frederick Crews, "The Power of Flannery O'Connor," *New York Review of Books* 37 (1990): 49–55; Claire Kahane, "The Maternal Legacy: The Grotesque Tradition in Flannery O'Connor's Female Gothic," in *The Female Gothic,* ed. Juliann Fleenor (Montreal: Eden Press, 1983); and Louise Westling, *Sacred Groves and Ravaged Gardens: The Fiction of Eudora Welty, Carson McCullers, and Flannery O'Connor* (Athens: University of Georgia Press, 1985).

2 In an earlier letter O'Connor expresses an equally wry sense of pleasure in this scene of mutilation: "I am very happy right now writing a story in which I plan for the heroine, aged 63, to be gored by a bull. I am not convinced yet that this is purgation or whether I identify myself with her or the bull. In any case, it is going to take some doing to do it and it may be the risk that is making me happy" (*HB* 129).

3 The list could go on and on: "Mrs. Watts's grin was as curved and sharp as the blade of a sickle. . . . Her eyes took everything in whole, like quicksand" (31); or, "She hit him across the legs with the stick, but he was like part of the tree" (33). The boundaries between animate and inanimate objects break down with uncanny frequency in O'Connor's prose. This boundary-breaking gives her prose an unexpected sadistic charge and gives her readers an anaesthetic "shock of the real."

4 It would be interesting to explore the scene where Hazel Motes runs over his double and survives, as well as the succeeding scene where the policeman destroys Hazel's car as translations of cartoon motifs into the stuff of high fiction.

5 O'Connor's prose evokes Kristeva's descriptions of the abject as "a violent, clumsy breaking away" from maternal power, "with the constant risk of falling back under the sway of a power as securing as it is stifling" (12–13).

6 To understand the full force of this tendency in O'Connor's prose, we would also need to analyze her ribald jokes and her outrageous sense of humor. In "Jokes," from *Rethinking Popular Culture*, ed. Chandra Mukerji and Michael Schudson (Berkeley: University of California Press, 1991), Mary Douglas suggests that "great rituals create unity in experience. They assert hierarchy and order. . . . But jokes have the opposite effect. They connect widely differing fields, but the connection destroys hierarchy and order. They do not affirm the dominant values, but denigrate and devalue. Essentially a joke is an anti-rite" (301). For Douglas the joke is a wonderful form of permitted aggression that has the salubrious effect of changing the balance of cultural power. O'Connor's humor challenges hierarchy and the standard-bearers of social control. It is a grown-up version of anti-angel aggression that needs to be even more fully explored.

7 As I've suggested, this portrait of woman as halted traveler is a recurring theme in O'Connor's fiction; someone we've already glimpsed in the scene where Hazel's mother is shut away in her coffin and the coffin lid cuts off "the light and the room" (13).

WORKS CITED

Adorno, Theodor W. *Negative Dialectics*. Trans. E. B. Ashton. New York: Continuum, 1983.

Notes To Literature, Vol. 1. Trans. Shierry Weber Nicholsen. New York: Columbia University Press, 1991.

Felman, Shoshana, and Dori Laub, M.D. *Testimony: Crises of Witnessing in Literature, Psychoanalysis, and History.* New York: Routledge, 1992.

Gilbert, Sandra M., and Susan Gubar. *The Madwoman in the Attic.* New Haven: Yale University Press, 1979.

Hansen, Miriam. "Of Mice and Ducks: Benjamin and Adorno on Disney." *South Atlantic Quarterly* 92 (1983).

Kahane, Claire. "Flannery O'Connor's Rage of Vision." *American Literature* 46 (1974).

Kristeva, Julia. *The Powers of Horror.* New York: Columbia University Press, 1982.

O'Connor, Flannery. *The Habit of Being.* Ed. Sally Fitzgerald. New York: Farrar, 1979.

Mystery and Manners. New York: Farrar, 1962.

Wise Blood (1952; rpt. New York: Farrar, Straus, Giroux, 1962.

Smith, Lillian. *Killers of the Dream.* New York: Norton, 1963.

Woolf, Virginia. *A Room of One's Own.* New York: Harcourt, 1981.

Zizek, Slavoj. *Enjoy Your Symptom: Jacques Lacan in Hollywood and out.* New York: Routledge, 1992.

The Sublime Object of Ideology. New York: Verso, 1991.

Notes on Contributors

Jon Lance Bacon received his Ph.D. in English from Vanderbilt University in 1991. He currently teaches English at Belmont University in Nashville. His book *Flannery O'Connor and Cold War Culture* was published by Cambridge University Press in 1993.

Robert H. Brinkmeyer, Jr., a Duke University B.A. and a University of North Carolina Ph.D., is currently Professor of English and Southern Studies at the University of Mississippi. His books include *Katherine Anne Porter's Artistic Development: Primitivism, Traditionalism, and Totalitarianism* (1993), *The Art and Vision of Flannery O'Connor* (1989), and *Three Catholic Writers of the Modern South* (1985).

Michael Kreyling is Professor of English at Vanderbilt. His books include *Eudora Welty's Vision of Order* (1980), *The Figure of the Hero in Southern Narrative* (1987), *Author and Agent: Eudora Welty and Diarmuid Russell* (1991).

James M. Mellard is Professor of English at Northern Illinois University. His books include *Using Lacan, Reading Fiction* (1991), *Doing Tropology: Analysis of Narrative Discourse* (1987), and *The Exploded Form: The Modernist Novel in America* (1980).

Patricia Smith Yaeger is Associate Professor of English at the University of Michigan, Ann Arbor. She is the author of *Honey-Mad Women: Emancipatory Strategies in Women's Writing* (1990) and co-editor of *Refiguring the Father: New Feminist Readings of Patriarchy* (1989).

A Note on the Text

Wise Blood, Flannery O'Connor's first novel, was originally published in 1952. A tenth anniversary edition, unchanged except for O'Connor's brief "Author's Note," was brought out in 1962, two years before the author's death. It is the 1962 text that we use in *New Essays.* It is available in *3 By Flannery O'Connor* (New York: New American Library, 1983), in *Wise Blood* (New York: Farrar, Straus & Giroux, 1962 [Noonday paperback]), and in *Flannery O'Connor: Collected Works* (New York: The Library of America, 1988).

Selected Bibliography

FICTION, ESSAYS, CORRESPONDENCE

Collected Works. New York: The Library of America, 1988.

The Complete Stories. New York: Farrar, Straus & Giroux, 1971.

The Correspondence of Flannery O'Connor and the Brainard Cheneys. Ed. C. Ralph Stephens. Jackson: University Press of Mississippi, 1986.

The Habit of Being [letters]. Ed. Sally Fitzgerald. New York: Farrar, Straus & Giroux, 1979.

Mystery and Manners [essays]. Ed. Sally Fitzgerald and Robert Fitzgerald. New York: Farrar, Straus & Giroux, 1969.

CRITICAL STUDIES

Asals, Frederick. *Flannery O'Connor: The Imagination of Extremity.* Athens: University of Georgia Press, 1982.

Brinkmeyer, Robert H., Jr. *The Art and Vision of Flannery O'Connor.* Baton Rouge: Louisiana State University Press, 1989.

Crews, Frederick. *The Critics Bear It Away: American Fiction and the Academy.* New York: Random House, 1992.

Desmond, John F. *Risen Sons: Flannery O'Connor's Vision of History.* Athens: University of Georgia Press, 1987.

Drake, Robert. *Flannery O'Connor: A Critical Essay.* [Grand Rapids, MI]: William P. Eerdmans, 1966.

Feeley, Sister Kathleen, S.S.N.D. *Flannery O'Connor: Voice of the Peacock.* New Brunswick, N.J.: Rutgers University Press, 1972.

Friedman, Melvin J., and Beverly Lyon Clark. *Critical Essays on Flannery O'Connor.* Boston: G. K. Hall, 1985. Critical essays on O'Connor's work covering several decades.

Hendin, Josephine. *The World of Flannery O'Connor.* Bloomington: Indiana University Press, 1970.

Mellard, James M. "Flannery O'Connor's *Others:* Freud, Lacan and the Unconscious." *American Literature.* 61 (December 1989): 624–43.

Montgomery, Marion. *Why Flannery O'Connor Stayed Home.* Chicago: Sherwood Sugden & Company, 1981.

Orvell, Miles. *Invisible Parade: The Fiction of Flannery O'Connor.* Philadelphia: Temple University Press, 1972.

Westling, Louise. *Sacred Groves and Ravaged Gardens: The Fiction of Eudora Welty, Carson McCullers, and Flannery O'Connor.* Athens: University of Georgia Press, 1985.

One film adaptation of the novel is available: *Wise Blood* (1979), directed by John Huston, screenplay by Benedict Fitzgerald.

Index